HOPE Stories

From the Bible

J.O.Terry

Encountering Orality in Disaster Response & Relief Ministry

Church Starting Network

"God is our refuge and strength,
an ever present help in trouble.
Therefore we will not fear,
though the earth give way
and the mountains fall into
the heart of the sea,
though its waters roar and foam
and the mountains quake
with their surging"
Psalm 46:1-3.

HOPE Stories

From the Bible

Copyright © 2009

By J.O.Terry

Requests for permission should be addressed to Church Starting Network, 3515 Sycamore School Road, Ft. Worth, Texas 76133.

Library of Congress Cataloging-in-Publication Data

J. O. Terry

ISBN 978-0-9825079-8-8

1. Bible Storying 2. Orality 3. People in need

Other Resources from
Church Starting Network

Church Starting and Growth

English

Daniel R. Sánchez, Ebbie C. Smith, and Curtis Watke, *Starting Reproducing Congregations: A Guidebook for Contextual New Church Development.* Ft. Worth, Texas: Church Starting Network, 2001.

Daniel R. Sánchez, Ebbie C. Smith, and Curtis Watke. *Starting Reproducing Congregations Strategy Planner: A Workbook for Contextual New Church Development.* Ft. Worth, Texas: Church Starting Network, 2001.

Ebbie C. Smith, *Growing Healthy Churches: New Directions for Church Growth in the 21st Century.* Ft. Worth, Texas: Church Starting Network, 2003.

Daniel R. Sánchez & Rudolofo González. *Sharing the Good News with Our Roman Catholic Friends.* Ft. Worth, Texas: Church Starting Network, 2004.

Daniel R. Sánchez, *Gospel in the Rosary.* Ft. Worth, Texas: Church Starting Network, 2004

Ebbie C. Smith. *Spiritual Warfare for 21st Century Christians.* Ft. Worth, Texas: Church Starting Network, 2005.

Daniel R. Sánchez, ed. *Church Planting Movements in North America.* Ft. Worth, Texas: Church Starting Network, 2007.

Daniel R. Sánchez, *Hispanic Realities Impacting America: Implications for Evangelism and Missions.* Ft. Worth, Texas: Church Starting Network,

Ebbie C. Smith, *Basic Churches are Real Churches.* Ft. Worth, Texas: Church Starting Network, 2009

Ebbie C. Smith, *You the Missionary: Committing to and Participating in God's Worldwide Mission.* Ft. Worth, Texas: Church Starting Network, 2009.

Spanish

Daniel R. Sánchez, Ebbie C. Smith, and Curtis Watke, *Como Sembrar Iglesias en el Siglo XXI.*

Daniel R. Sánchez, Ebbie C. Smith, and Curtis Watke, *Mis Planes Estratégicos Para Sembrar Iglesias en El Siglo XXI: Libro de trabajo para el desarrollo contextual de una iglesia nueva.* Ft. Worth, Texas: Church Starting Network, 2002.

Daniel R. Sánchez & Ebbie C. Smith, *Cultivando Iglesias Saludables.* Ft. Worth, Texas: Church Starting Network, 2008.

Daniel R. Sánchez & Rodolfo González. *Comparta Las Buenas Nuevas Con Sus Amigos Católicos.* Ft. Worth, Texas: Church Starting Network, 2004.

Daniel R. Sánchez. *Evangelio En El Rosario.* Ft. Worth, Texas: Church Starting Network, 2004.

Daniel R. Sánchez. *Iglesia: Crecimiento y Cultura.* Ft. Worth, Texas: Church Starting Network, 2004.

Daniel R. Sánchez. *Manual para Implementar Crecimiento y Cultura.* Ft. Worth, Texas: Church Starting Network, 2004.

Daniel R. Sánchez. *Realidades Hispanas Que Impacta A América: Implicaciones para Evangelización y Misiones.* Ft. Worth, Texas: Church Starting Network, 2006.

J.O. Terry, *Guía Para La Narrativa Bíblica* (Synopsis of the Bible Storying Handbook, translated into Spanish by Keith Stamps). Ft. Worth, Texas: Church Starting Network, 2008.

Bible Storying Resources

J.O Terry, *Basic Bible Storying*. Ft. Worth, Texas: Church Starting Network, 2006.

Daniel R. Sánchez, J.O. Terry, LaNette Thompson. *Bible Storying for Church Planting*. Ft. Worth, Texas: Church Starting Network, 2008.

J.O. Terry, *Bible Storying Handbook: For Short-Term Church Mission Teams and Mission Volunteers*. Ft. Worth, Texas: Church Starting Network, 2008.

J.O. Terry, *Guía Para La Narrativa Bíblica* (Synopsis of the Bible Storying Handbook, translated into Spanish by Keith Stamps). Ft. Worth, Texas: Church Starting Network, 2008.

J.O. Terry, *Hope Stories from the Bible*. Ft. Worth, Texas: Church Starting Network, 2008.

Daniel R. Sánchez and J.O. Terry. *LifeStory Encounters*. Ft. Worth, Texas: Church Starting Network, 2009.

J. O. Terry, *Death Stories from the Bible*. Ft. Worth, Texas: Church Starting Network, 2009.

J. O. Terry, *Food Stories from the Bible*. Ft. Worth, Texas: Church Starting Network, 2009.

J. O. Terry, *Grief Stories from the Bible*. Ft. Worth, Texas: Church Starting Network, 2009.

J. O. Terry, *Water Stories from the Bible*. Ft. Worth: Church Starting Network, 2009.

The Church Starting Network supplies all of these resources:

www.ChurchStarting.net

3515 Sycamore School Road, Fort Worth, Texas 76133

Contents

Chapter 1

Background

Newscasts almost daily announce tragedies and the suffering that beset people around the world. These sufferings and anxieties stem from disasters that occur as the result of accidents, disease, drought, earthquakes, famine, floods, poverty, storms, terrorist activities, or war. When facing these bad things, need *hope* in addition to physical relief that seeks to alleviate their immediate suffering and facilitate a return to a safe and normal life. Responders who minister to these suffering masses in this world have long recognized the need for one or more sets of Bible stories that could be used for comforting people. These same times of crisis provide opportunities to remind people of God's love and care for them in this life as well as God's great desire to forgive their sins through the Savior Jesus and prepare them for the life to come.

People are often more open to the gospel during times of deep crisis when their world is turned upside down. Those who share the Gospel may not, however, have the opportunity to present a complete Old Testament foundation and then a generous number of the stories of Jesus needed to lead listeners to saving faith in Jesus as Savior. The confusion and distraction of a local situation may prohibit a longer and more in-depth Bible Storying strategy. People have a more immediate need of comfort and hope. This comfort and hope leading to peace helps to soothe their emotional wounds brought about by their immediate situation. Hope can also open the door to a later more thorough evangelistic presentation using Bible stories that permit listeners to make an informed decision to believe in Jesus as Savior and Lord. Suffering people can more readily hear the message of Jesus and reflect on it when they are not so pre-occupied with their losses and daily physical needs.

The Bible Storyer needs a handy pocket-sized set of HOPE Bible stories that provides a broad spectrum of stories reminding listeners they live in God's world where He alone is sovereign, compassionate, loving, and powerful. These stories should remind the people that God is able to help in time of need. When the storyer shares stories of hope and comfort, only minimal need exists for a lengthy post-story discussion as in a typical storying session. However, the storying sessions might benefit from including a few think-about-it questions or non-structured discussions just to provide an opening for listeners to interact with the story and possibly relate to it in some way. As always, a memory verse keyed to hope and God's deliverance should also aid in initiating response.

The storyer also will likely be serving as a relief worker. He or she will likely be tired and preoccupied with the daily work. Consequently, lengthy preparation of highly detailed lessons is not a typical option. What is needed is a compact set of stories that can be used quickly and simply. To that end, I share this set of HOPE Stories.

The stories are prepared with prayer. The storyers will need to energize the stories with their prayer as they tell them. All glory and credit goes to our Heavenly Father for His generous portion of Bible stories demonstrating God's great love and compassion for hurting and needy people. Storyers can choose from these suggested stories or add others more appropriate to their people and as time and opportunity permit. These Bible stories are presented generally in a chronological order, but this does not mean they must be told in this same order. The mix of stories includes those for both men and women. If additional stories are required, The HOPE Stories can serve as model of how to develop additional stories from the Bible version used locally. Storyers are encouraged to make any necessary adaptation to the stories as needed for their listeners. The stories and discussion materials developed by storyers in specific situations are uniquely tailored for their own typical ministry situations. Finally, allow the Holy Spirit to anoint and empower the storying in preparation and telling.

In the event that listeners are moved to consider believing in Christ as Savior, a story is included leading to invitation to do so. For others who need more time, any of the already developed evangelistic Bible Storying models could be introduced at a later time. After the time of crisis, when stability has returned, the good will earned through the disaster response may well lead to an openness and relationship with listeners to hear more stories selected especially for evangelism and discipleship.

All Scripture used is from the New International Version unless otherwise noted. Line drawing illustrations are from "Telling the Story..."[1] illustrations by Caloy Gabuco and published jointly by International Mission Board, SBC, and New Tribes Mission.

Additional Bible story sets are available. *The Water Stories*[2] was initially developed for use with water projects which included digging or sinking wells and installing hand pumps, constructing water reservoirs, and surface water filtering and purification systems. These are stories from the Bible that speak about thirst, washing and cleansing, and the living water of salvation. Some of these might be helpful to use.

Another set originally developed for use among Muslim women is popularly called *Grief Stories*[3] and consists of selected stories of Bible women and the misfortunes they suffered and how God redeemed their lives. *Water Stories* and *Grief Stories* have subtle evangelistic themes leading to opportunity for drawing the net.

Another set of stories still in preparation is *Food Stories*[4] pointing to the Bread from Heaven that satisfies the hunger of the soul. This one too will have a subtle evangelistic theme leading to opportunity to draw the net.

HOPE Stories is the result of requests dating back to the 1970s for suitable ministry resources to use along with survival and health resources that were for ready use whenever disasters occurred. During the intervening years there were many incidences of ministry shared during disaster response times, but no story sets were prepared in a ready form for sharing with others.

This writer was invited during 2004 to teach basic Bible Storying concepts suitable for use during disaster response at the Disaster Assistance Response Training (DART)[5] in Bartlesville, OK, conducted by Strategic World Impact ministries. In preparation for the breakout sessions the collection of commonly used ministry stories were compiled and shared digitally as *HOPE Stories*.

The preparation and sharing of this story set happened early in the year before the tsunami devastated many areas in Southeast and South Asia later that same year. There was an immediate need for an appropriate ministry resource for use while volunteer workers labored to aid the victims. Later, when the tragic earthquake occurred in Pakistan, another request came for appropriate ministry aids. Similar ministry response needs have since arisen with volunteer workers asking for resource materials to comfort and provide hope while building a relationship that would open opportunity for a more direct evangelistic witness in God's time.

I share this book to partially satisfy these needs. I apologize for any shortcomings the user may encounter. But if this effort stimulates, directs, and aids potential response workers in preparing their own HOPE Stories, I will consider my effort rewarded.

Readers already familiar with Bible Storying, will apply their knowledge of storying in general to the specific application of telling HOPE Stories. Others who do not have a background in Bible Storying might profit from a study of Chapters 3, 4, and 6 that describe the basic considerations for story preparation, telling the stories and drawing the net at the conclusion of the stories. The same guidance is given in far more complete form in the author's book, *Basic Bible Storying*.[6]

Chapter 2

Encountering Orality

A Rationale

Those who must learn by listening because of a lack of literacy, or who simply prefer to learn by listening are everywhere. We call these people *oral learners* or *oral communicators*. They live in cultures where stories have primary value for entertaining, educating, instructing, motivating, comforting, and inspiring. To reach the minds and hearts of these people may require, in addition to acts of kindness and friendship during their time of need, verbal expressions of hope that endure beyond the time of crisis. A powerful method to provide these verbal expressions best is through the form of stories, especially Bible stories which speak of God's love, provision, and his omnipotent power to save, heal, and restore.

To make best use of the Bible stories, it is helpful to understand some of the general characteristics of oral learners. One must be aware of the difference between oral learners and people like ourselves who are most likely adequately literate. Space does not allow a complete review all the available information on orality. This writer learned about orality when, as a literate Western-culture Christian, he encountered orality among deep rural and tribal peoples in South Asian countries. After initial failure to engage and teach these oral learners effectively, working with them helped to understand how they perceive new information, learn from it, remember it for later recall, and act upon new information coming from an outside source.

Characteristics of
Oral Learners

For responders the use of Bible stories as an accompaniment to ministry is a new venture. To better prepare for encountering orality during crisis and relief ministries,

Christian workers are well advised to take time to review some of the typical characteristics of oral learners. Doing so will benefit the responder by preparing him/her to communicate more effectively, not only in the immediate ministry to disaster victims, but also to leave a scriptural legacy as the people continue to reflect on the stories and share the stories among their people. The benefits of the storying encounter will, therefore, endure and be shared widely.

Characteristics of Oral Learners

1. Thoughts are retained as memorable events to be described in narrative accounts rather than as specific descriptive words.
2. Communication is generally copious and redundant using many words and often repeating thoughts.
3. Events are often remembered by time markers—simultaneous significant events—rather than the clock or calendar date.
4. People enjoy learning *en group*, that is, in the company of others that heightens their learning experience.
5. Oral learners enjoy learning participatively ranging from catechism to inductive discussion, repetition, singing, and often through role-playing or drama. Best teaching comes from leading listeners to learn actively rather than "teaching at them."
6. Oral learners are usually very relational — they must develop some kind of satisfactory relationship with their teacher and be comfortable in the presence of their peers. And they learn best if they can relate to the stories in some way.
7. Curiosity is often a characteristic of oral learners but is balanced by the fact that they live in societies where little new or different happens—every day is like every other day.
8. Oral learners can mentally tire easily as they likely are not used to taking in large amounts of new information and assimilating it, especially information that is difficult to relate to immediately, or that no immediate value is realized.
9. Not all oral learners have verbatim memory; in fact, most need to hear things several times for a good memory to develop.
10. It is not uncommon for oral learners to alter new information to fit their expectation or be consistent with their social or cultural norms or existing beliefs. New information is passed through their cultural-oral window.
11. Narratives in the form of stories form new information

containers for oral learners enabling them to more easily receive and retain and pass that information along to others. Stories that are linked or related as part of a cluster or series tend to better anchor or stabilize individual stories.

12. Change for oral learners may only come after the new stories fill in gaps in their present knowledge or change their present beliefs by presenting better beliefs or a weightier coherent story than their story.

Oral learners manifest other general characteristics as well as many specific to different cultures. What is important is for the Bible storyer to be patient and observant to learn from their listeners how the listeners prefer to learn. The storyer will always begin with some assumptions, but needs to be prepared to adjust storying style and any accompanying teaching style as needed and preferred by their listeners.

Teaching oral learners demands repetition as often as listeners desire. Repetition can be both by the storyer and by the listeners if they are willing to retell the stories during the sessions. The basic strategy of Bible Storying requires that communicators develop sets of Bible stories that will meet the needs enough for listeners to gain a basic sense of the Bible's teaching. Oral learners are very relational as a general rule so will respond best to stories they can sense a relationship with, either the event in the story, or the characters. The sets of stories should also seek to react to and to overcome any significant worldview or cultural issues that may hinder understanding, believing, or acting on the intent of the Bible stories.

To achieve the ends of communicating the biblical truth and overcoming cultural barriers to understanding, storyers should employ as many stories as practical, fitting the time frame of opportunity and enough for the listeners to "come on board" by relating to the stories. Storyers should not limit the stories for his/her own convenience. Storyers should seek to balance relational stories (those similar to listeners' culture and everyday life) to those with specific spiritual truths leading to salvation. The object is to keep listeners listening as long as possible until there is evidence of response or change prompted by the Holy Spirit. Be patient with oral learners and persevere while accommodating their preferred learning style.

I had to learn that oral learners do things intuitively on one hand and out of ritual, habit or community expectation on the other. This often meant that I could not get someone to explain why they did what they did. They did it because "that was what one should do." For many that I trained to use Bible stories, I gave them exposure to more stories than they probably needed but which I estimated they needed to hear. Then those being trained would intuitively select and use certain stories they felt were best for their people. In time I learned to anticipate more of their decisions but was never able to know for sure why.

Since most live in highly relational communal societies the role of relationship to story characters, to story events and to consequences or outcome is relatively high. Though there seems to be a tipping point that needs to be reached at times, and, unless it is reached, the relationship factor may not manifest. In terms of using Bible stories this can mean that several stories which have a common truth or teaching may be needed to find the most relational story.

Also for the storyer this can mean that a number of stories might need telling before the listeners accept the storyer or find some basis to relate to the storyer. I often used a simple personal story or two to help my listeners find a way to relate to me. My mother grew up on a farm where I spent some my early of summers. I found that farm stories often related well. Also stories of how I related to certain family members seemed interesting to listeners. After spending time with a group and going away to work elsewhere and later returning to the group, I found that if I recalled things that had happened when I was with them earlier, this was a great way to rekindle relationship.

For a good in-depth article on orality see Rick Brown's article "Communicating God's Word in an Oral Culture" in the International Journal of Frontier Missions, vol 21/3. http://www.ijfm.org/archives.htm.

Chapter 3

Preparing to Tell Bible Stories

Persons who are new to the concept of Bible Storying must accept and implement the truth that storying involves commitment to preparation. The idea that a storyer already knows the Bible stories and therefore needs little preparation is a vastly unwise conclusion. The storyer must accept the necessity of careful preparation and familiarity with the stories, even to being able to tell them without an open Bible or notes.

Stories are meant to be told and are best learned so they can be told with a reasonable degree of fluency. It is quite possible that many readers will be working through an interpreter so the local people can understand in their own language. In such cases, the storyer will find it helpful to prepare the stories well with a view to expressing the stories so the interpreters can clearly understand the stories and share them in the heart language of the listeners.

This book later suggests some typical stories to use that in many ways illustrate God's concern and provision for the needs of the people in that day. The book will also suggest stories that show the compassion of Jesus during his days of ministry in Palestine. Storyers will be alert to recall other Bible stories that speak in definite relational ways to the listeners being served.

Using Model Stories

Model stories have great value in developing and providing a thematic concept and contributing starting ideas for preparing the storyer's own story set that is most appropriate for his/her listeners. Model story sets, such as *The HOPE Stories*, can, however, lead the new storyer to a lack of preparation where he/she simply takes the model stories and, without any real investment in preparation, attempts to use the stories *as is*. Some new to Bible Storying have even tried to use the representative discussion questions whether they were appropriate or not for their particular listeners.

This caution is not to say that this set is not appropriate for your ministry needs. It may be. But take the time to study your intended listeners online or via correspondence with those already living or working in the area where you will go to ministry. Ask about vocabulary restrictions, preferences, cultural and spiritual issues that may be confronted in some of the stories. Also ask about the places or times when it is appropriate or possible to tell Bible stories.

Using Bible Stories in Ministry

After living in the Asia Pacific Region for 35 years, I can say that I have seen more than my share of disasters and relief ministry needs. All of these disasters produced great physical stress within the population as well as bringing question into the peoples' minds, "Why did this happen to me?" Following each disaster or relief need was a time of deep emotional wounding and spiritual emptiness. It is a time when many of the victims said: "Our gods have failed us. Where can we turn for help?"

Following the terrible cyclone disaster in Orissa, India, (south of Calcutta) the lowland Hindus experienced great destruction and loss of property. Some of the Kui tribals, who are Christians, came out of the mountains to help repair and rebuild the destroyed farms and homes. The lowlanders asked: "Why are you doing this for us?"

Many of those Kui tribals had been earlier trained to use Bible stories to witness and minister. Radical Hindus had for years directed severe persecution toward Christians and caused trouble for any persons caught carrying a Bible under their arms. A previous tribal training program had urged the men to learn the stories and not carry a Bible as they went to help with agriculture projects.

10

In yet another case in Western India following a severe earthquake no one was prepared to go to the families who had suffered great loss and death of loved ones. No one was prepared to comfort the families and assure them that there was a God who loved them and who was powerful to help and change their circumstances. I was invited to train some Indian workers afterward to be better prepared for ministering and comforting listeners in future disasters.

For years some of us had sought to be prepared to tell appropriate Bible stories during the times when people experienced disaster. This effort had never been well organized. The result was sort of hit and miss in the selection of Bible stories to accompany other teaching about purifying water and good sanitation. Sometime stories that were used following a disaster were interesting to hear but did not relate well to immediate need for spiritual and emotional comfort. Other stories like the "Feeding of the Multitude" did fit well as they told of being able to eat until satisfied, often where adequate food was the major need. The "Parable of the Great Banquet" in which those invited to a rich banquet spurned the invitation even as the food was prepared and ready to be served was mind-boggling to those who seldom get enough to eat. And from a cultural viewpoint they saw how the invited guests dishonored their host by refusing the invitation. For many listeners this story makes a good transition to an invitation to believe—God has prepared the banquet of salvation and all are invited. Who will accept and who will refuse the invitation?

Selecting Bible Stories

One of my basic reasons for preparing the story models was to answer the question: Which stories should I tell? The story collections are not meant to limit in any way the choice of other stories deemed more appropriate or relative to local need. These are just models to suggest what one could do and to help and encourage potential storyers to be prepared to tell Bible stories when the need or opportunity arises. I've used these stories that represent what I would typically find appropriate in these situations. It is not necessary or even possible most times to tell all the stories or even to tell them in chronological order. Story sets like these are basically thematically organized rather than chronologically organized. So storyers can pick and choose or simply be prepared and let the Holy Spirit direct when opportunity arises. As you read and study your Bible keep a notebook to list other stories that you think might have value. Note the theme of the story and the need and how God or Jesus resolved the need.

Preparing Stories

Many of the Bible stories are good to go *as is* in that they are fairly straightforward and not overly complicated. The "Bartimaeus Story" is a good example of a simple story that needs no crafting to make it a good oral narrative. But other stories might need some preparation or "crafting" to make them better oral narratives. Most of the narratives are "tellable" *as is* with only minor adapting.

Unfamiliar details or proper names of people or places not well identified in a story can be confusing to listeners who do not know the story and may never have opportunity to read it. Moreover those geographical names or names of various people groups mentioned in the stories often mean little to people hearing Bible stories for the first time. I suggest, therefore, that storyers simplify the stories appropriately to keep a focus on the main characters and events and not to overload a listener with details they cannot understand. Those in literacy work suggest keeping the proper names in a given story to three unless others are already known from previous stories. Obviously, rules are made to be broken, so this is just a guideline. You can always check it out by telling a story with many proper names in it and then asking a listener to retell the same story and listen to see how many names are retained in their story.

Dialog between characters is the lifeblood of most Bible stories. I once mistakenly over simplified Bible stories by removing most of the character dialog and just narrated what happened. I learned the hard way that the stories delivered in this manner were lifeless and uninteresting. In fact, there is the possibility that the story characters can say things that would get you or me stoned by some listeners if we were attempting to teach that, but often the story characters can say it in their dialog. The words are their words, not ours!

Pronoun/antecedent displacement. Another aspect of dialog is to be careful about too many pronouns getting displaced from proper nouns. In some translations of the Gospel of Mark in chapter five it goes something like this:

> "They went across the lake to the region of the Gerasenes. When he got out of the boat a man with an evil spirit came from the tombs to meet him. He lived in the tombs, and no one could bind him anymore, not even with a chain. He had often been chained hand and foot but he tore the chains apart and broke the irons on his feet."

We know the first "he" refers to Jesus but the listeners might not understand this. So it would be better to say: "When *Jesus* got out of the boat a man with an evil spirit came from the tombs to meet *Jesus. The man* lived in the tombs...." In this way the listeners can clearly distinguish between the characters. Also I might add that I would begin with: "Jesus and his disciples went across the lake to another region." You get the idea since listeners would not know what "Gerasenes" was. This may seem very redundant to you to repeat these proper names so often. But it will help to keep the interpreter clear on who is saying or doing what, and for the listeners, who do not know the story, to follow it clearly. The first couple of times you do this in a story may seem awkward, but it gets easier. Remember the Bible was edited for good reading and your story needs crafting for good telling.

Keep sentences relatively short and uncomplicated. Longer sentences may need breaking down into shorter ones. Avoid dependent clauses as these are both more difficult to translate and to follow by listeners who have a practice of speaking more directly and simply. Descriptive words are

13

good to use, but like seasoning, use reasonably. Oral communicators use "and" to connect things. The Gospel of Mark bears evidence of being an "oral gospel." Notice how the story connects one event with another.

Long Bible stories are more of a challenge to keep the story reasonable in length and moving. The Jonah story can be summed up in ten verses but, of course, it is much more interesting with the additional details. Later on you will see what I did with the Ruth story in "A Husband and Son for a Faithful Widow."

Numbers, especially large numbers, pose problems for many oral learners. In their own communication it is common for them to refer to large numbers in some concrete manner. In the Bible stories Abraham was to have descendants like the *stars in the sky* or *sands along the seashore*. In the Flood Story it may be enough to say that God told Noah how large to build the ark rather than giving the dimensions. Notice how many numbers are in that story. Could we say that after it rained for forty days and nights that the waters remained on the earth a long time, or nearly a year.

Another issue may be the names of God used in a story. I get caught by this all the time. A story may refer to *God* and at other time to *the Lord*. Be consistent and be aware that in some situations it might be best to use *Lord Jehovah* or *Jehovah God* to give a name and not just a title. This may or may not be a problem as local Bible translations have usually taken this into account.

Write out your stories in the same form as you would tell them. To learn how to do this, tell a story, record it, and then write down what you said in telling the story. Test your stories if you are not sure. Sometimes my interpreters were kind to help me express a story better for their people. And I also learned from how the listeners expressed the story after they had heard it. For more on story selection and story crafting see the text *Basic Bible Storying*.

Chapter 4

Telling Bible Stories

Some consider the most challenging factor in Bible Storying relates to knowing how and when to engage the listeners in stories. For others this may come naturally. However, there are some things to consider which may help to open up opportunities for sharing one or more Bible stories.

In general training related to Bible Storying use and strategies I share the concept of a *Bible Storying Toolbox*. Really this is an encouragement to think creatively as you actively search out opportunities when people are gathered or available for hearing a story.

Strategies for Storying

Let me suggest a few of these methods.

Share Stories With National Co-workers

This is the most obvious opportunity for beginning to tell stories. In the evening when the work for the day is done and relief workers and national co-workers are gathered to eat, rest and plan for the next day, it is a good time to share the stories in the group. But be sure to do this in a place and loudly enough for others among the people group to hear. Sometimes a bit of singing first will attract listeners who are curious. When the onlookers begin to gather, begin the stories. Two or three in one session is a good number. If you plan to use some of the discussion questions, these can be done rhetorically in which you ask the question as a think-about-it item and then after a pause proceed to answer the question. Or, ask the question and wait to see if someone responds with an answer. Caution your international colleagues to let the other listeners respond if they will.

Man of Peace Strategy

One effective strategy in storying is sometimes called the *Man of Peace Strategy*. This strategy begins when the storyer visits with people. The people might ask where will you spend the night or where will you eat. They will then sometimes offer hospitality. This offer opens up a communal opportunity to share. When this happens in the relaxed atmosphere of eating or visiting, the host will sometimes ask what do you do. One response you can make is, "I am a storyteller."

In my experience this has often led hosts to ask, "What kind of stories do you tell?" Then I can have the floor to share some of the stories I know. I always begin wide and progressively move toward the specific. Creation is a good "wide" beginning. Stories where Jesus helps people are more specific as they relate to various needs. However, remember that you may be asked if you have another story, or what comes next? So have several stories in mind and practiced for easy recall and sharing. If this is difficult to do, then have some pre-recorded.

Situational Storying

A second strategy is situational storying. It most often relates to the opportunity arising from a situation or ministry event. One scenario that has happened many times is an invitation to visit a home to pray for some family member who is sick or injured. When this has happened I have told the gathered family and neighbors that I will pray in the name of Jesus who came from heaven and taught us how to pray and to always pray in his name. Then I say: May I tell you a story about this Jesus before I pray? I tell one of the stories that I feel is most appropriate (as led by the Holy Spirit). Then pray for the person. Upon departing ask peace and a blessing upon the home or those gathered and offer to tell more stories if invited back again.

During Relief Projects

The Water Stories was prepared for use during clean water projects when water was the topic and people were gathered to watch the work. I always look for some opening like asking the people if they have ever been thirsty, really thirsty, and longed for a drink of clean fresh water. Then I continue with: "I have some stories about thirsty people and wells and water that truly satisfies."

For others, ritual purity is a concern so stories like *Naaman the Leper* or the leper who begged Jesus to heal him can have appeal. At a meal, storyers may use the *Parable of the Great Banquet* where the invitation was refused or the *Feeding of the Multitude*, or even *The Prodigal Son* who returned home and his father called for a feast to be prepared. Look for themes that relate to the moment.

Fast-Track Storying

Let me mention one additional possibility where a continuous story is told that ties together many stories. We call this *Fast-Track Storying* because it continues by bridging from story to story without stopping for any comment or discussion. Usually the stories are compressed a bit without the many details or full dialog that a single story might use.

To do this means that you select a series of stories which can logically be told as a continuing story by bridging from story to story. While this may not be typically appropriate for a disaster response time I often do a *Fast-Track Story* of the Passion story beginning with Jesus' entry into Jerusalem and ending with the Ascension and the words of the angels about the return of Jesus. A representative series of the ministry stories of Jesus is good to prepare for use.

Use Puppets

Some teams have used hand puppets like Muppets to tell their stories or to interact with the stories. Puppets are an acceptable form of adult entertainment in many Asian cultures. It is an interesting thing that puppets can often say things that would get the storyer in trouble. Of course, the storyer is the one telling the story, but use of the puppet seems to provide some entertaining distancing for story content that may be confrontational or perceived otherwise in a hostile attitude.

Pre-Recoded Stories

Pre-recorded stories in English where it can be understood or the local language can be played on a cassette player or a digital device like that from *MegaVoice*.[7] The volume of the MegaVoice Ambassador is loud enough for a small group to listen comfortably. One group cleverly played the stories from a cassette in a local language and then asked one of the listeners who also spoke English to tell them what was being said. IPODs and small battery powered speakers also work great. The stories can play while other work is being done. Teaching programs can be interspersed among stories or can lead into the stories. Typically teaching about clean water and oral rehydration are common parallel topics.

Play Recorded Stories in Clinic Waiting Areas

The Bible stories can be played or even told live over and over again. Pre-recorded stories in the national language have the advantage of not being interrupted for interpretation. And after the relief project is ended the recordings can be left behind with a trusted person. Compact Discs are great as they cannot be over-recorded.

Some Practical Matters

Take a Bible or not? Do you take a Bible with you? Maybe, maybe not. In some places possession of a Bible may jeopardize your work or even your freedom to remain in the area. Such limitations mean that you need to learn the stories and practice telling them before going. Where appropriate I have used some picture sets to sort of cue me on what to tell next. The practice of outlining your stories just as you would tell them has proved to be a good way to begin. Usually after 3-5 tellings you own the story and don't need your notes any more.

Read or recite stories—Stories can also be read or "recited" from an open Bible if this encourages acceptance as true stories. Stories should be read slowly and with emphasis as if being told. Remember to be careful about how you handle a Bible in the presence of listeners who have a deep respect for a "holy book." I had to work with interpreters who were also reading a story or portions of it to read slowly and clearly and with expression. One of the difficulties I ran into in some countries is that the local language, for instance Bengali, was a poetic literary language. And holy books like the Bible were then written in a "high language" and not in a vernacular common to speaking. And some forms of reading are closer to chanting than to interpretative reading. Obviously, this works best when English can be used or if responders can speak and read the local language. A read story in such situations should always be followed by a told story that is in the everyday vernacular. Reading the story "anchors" it in the Bible. Telling the story "anchors" it in the head and heart.

One Bible storyer in Central America remarked that many of the mother tongue peoples like Mayans liked for religious services and teachings to have an aura of mystery or "loftiness" to them rather than in plain language. Since many oral communicators live in animistic cultures they sense power in words they do not know and expressions they cannot understand. Words written on a piece of paper which they may not be able to read are deemed powerful and sometimes chewed and swallowed to obtain power or some blessing or protection.

Don't worry about repeating the same stories—People in oral cultures generally enjoy hearing stories again. Sometimes they enjoy the story better the second or third time as by then they know the story or have caught parts of it they missed in earlier tellings.

Don't be afraid to make mistakes—you will make them anyway. Bible Storying skill develops as you do it. The first time I had an all-day storying session I sweated blood, holding the Bible in one hand and a book of Bible story lessons in the other. In time, I learned to let go of the storybook and only use the Bible. Then one dark night in a village without electricity and only a flickering oil lamp I learned to let go of the Bible as a crutch as well. I made a few mistakes in my story but I was liberated! Though a bit out of practice now since leaving the mission field, I learned to tell stories from memory all day or in whatever time frame I had.

Tell the story from the story—It helps to "stand in the story" and tell what you see happening and hear being said by those around you in the story. It helps you to visualize the story and remember it better. Once you learn a story well this is easier to do. It is not uncommon for oral learners to see the story happening right there before them as a living story, alive at that very moment and not a dead story from long ago. The storyer can help to make this happen by telling the story as though it were happening right then.

Let your body help tell the story—John Walsh, a professional storyteller, reminds that it is good to involve your whole body in body positioning, gestures, facial expressions, and voice inflection so that the whole body learns the story. Then your body can help your mind to tell the story!

One last thought is to always tell your stories from the overflow in your own life. Learn the stories, live with the stories, enjoy telling the stories, and cultivate an attitude of needing to share your stories with someone. "I have a story that has blessed (or helped) me very much, let me tell you the story so you will be blessed, too." After all, you are telling about your Heavenly Father and his great love and about Jesus your Savior.

Chapter 5

Stories of Hope for Those
In Need of God's Help

HOPE Stories

1. When God Clothed the Naked

Scripture Base: Genesis 2-3; Isaiah 61:10; 64:6

Stir Their Thinking:

1. What is it like to discover that you are naked? Is there shame?
2. If you were found naked, who would take pity on you and provide clothing?
3. Who could provide the best clothing to cover your nakedness?

Tell the Story:

When God Clothed the Naked

In the beginning when the world was created it was God who created the first man and woman. God made the man from the dust of the earth and breathed into him the breath of life. Then God placed the man in a garden and gave the man work to care for the garden. There God made all kinds of trees to grow—trees that were pleasing to the eye and good for food. Among the trees was a tree called the tree of the knowledge of good and evil. God commanded the man: "You must not eat from the tree of the knowledge of good and evil, for when you eat of it you will surely die."

God saw that the man was alone with no suitable companion. So God caused the man to fall into a deep sleep and while the man was sleeping God removed bone and flesh and from them made woman. Then God brought the woman to the man who was pleased. The man and his wife were both naked and they felt no shame.

One day the serpent, who was craftier than any of the other wild animals, said to the woman: "Did God really say, 'You must not eat from any tree in the garden?'"

The woman replied, "We may eat from the trees in the garden, but God did say, 'You must not eat fruit from the tree that is in the middle of the garden, and you must not touch it, or you will die."

The serpent answered, "You will not surely die. God knows that when you eat of that tree your eyes will be opened, and you will be wise like God, knowing good and evil."

When the woman saw that the fruit of the tree was good for food and pleasing to the eye, and also desirable for gaining wisdom, she took some and ate it. The woman also gave some fruit to her husband, who was with her, and he also ate the fruit. Then the eyes of both the woman and her husband were opened, and they realized they were naked and became ashamed and sewed leaves together to make coverings for their nakedness.

When God came in the cool of the day to walk and talk with the man and woman they had hidden themselves among the trees of the garden. The man said, "I heard you in the garden, I was afraid because I was naked, so I hid."

God judged the man and woman because they disobeyed His command. Then God made clothing for the man and his wife from the skins of animals and so he clothed them. Afterward God banished the man and woman from the garden so they would now have to till the soil to grow their food. That is the story from God's Word the Bible.

Comfort the Heart:

1. When God made the man and woman and they were naked, were they ashamed?

2. When did the man and woman become ashamed?
3. What did they try to do to cover their nakedness and shame? Do you think that was a lasting clothing?
4. Was God concerned about the man and woman's nakedness and shame?
5. What did God provide for the man and woman to cover their nakedness? Was that a better clothing for their shame?
6. There are other stories that tell about even better clothing that God will provide for all who believe in the Anointed One God sent to suffer shame on our account. For God says that all our righteousness (good deeds) are as filthy rags before a holy and righteous God (Isa 64:6).

Remember the Blessing:

"I delight greatly in the Lord; my soul rejoices in my God. For he has clothed me with garments of salvation and arrayed me in a robe of righteousness" (Isaiah 61:10a).

"The man and his wife heard the sound of the LORD God as he was walking in the garden in the cool of the day, and they

hid from the LORD God among the trees of the garden"
(Genesis 3:8).

HOPE Stories

2. When God Saved a Family

Scripture Base: Genesis 6:5-9:17; Matthew 24:37-38; Luke 17:26-27

Stir Their Thinking:

1. When floods come how do you escape? Who could help you to safety until the flood passed?
2. There was a time long ago when there was great wickedness and evil on the earth. God warned a man that a great flood was coming and told the man what he must do to prepare to escape death in the flood.
3. The man believed God's warning and obeyed what he was told to do to save his family and animals.

Tell the Story:

When God Saved a Family

Long ago there was a time when there was great wickedness and evil on the earth. God who had created all things saw this wickedness and evil and was grieved in his heart. God said, "I will destroy mankind, whom I have created from the face of the earth—men and animals, and all creatures and birds. But there was a man named Noah who found favor in God's eyes for he was a righteous man who was blameless among the people of his day. God was pleased with Noah because Noah walked with God—living a life pleasing to God.

Noah had three sons who were also married.

So God said to Noah, "I am surely going to destroy the wicked people for I am going to bring floodwaters on the earth to destroy all life under heaven, every creature that has the breath of life in it. Everything on earth will perish. So make yourself a boat of wood and coat it with pitch inside and out. I will establish my covenant with you. You and your

25

wife and your sons and their wives are to enter the boat along with all the animals that I bring to you." Then God told Noah how large to build the boat and to take all the necessary food for Noah's family and all the animals. Noah did everything just as God commanded him to do.

When the boat was completed God said to Noah, "Go into the boat, you and your whole family, because I have found you righteous among your people. Seven days from now I will send rain on the earth for forty days and forty nights and destroy every living creature." Then Noah and his family and all the animals entered the boat and God closed the door. Noah did all that God commanded him.

In that day before the flood, people were eating and drinking, marrying and being given in marriage, up to the day that Noah and his family entered the boat to escape the flood. The people knew nothing about what would happen until the flood came and took them all away.

The floodwaters rose steadily until at last all the earth was covered and everything with the breath of life in it perished. Only Noah and those with him in the boat were safe from the flood. After a long time had passed God remembered Noah and his family and all the animals. So God sent a wind over the earth to dry up the water. After many days had passed Noah sent out a raven and it kept flying back and forth but did not return. Then Noah sent out a dove but it could find no place to rest and so returned. Again Noah sent out the dove and this time it returned with a freshly plucked green leaf in its beak. Then God said to Noah, "Come out of the boat, you and your wife and your sons and their wives. Bring out all the animals, too."

Noah built an altar and offered a sacrifice to God for saving him and his family and the animals. God was pleased with the sacrifice and said, "Never again will I curse the ground because of man, even though their hearts are filled with evil. Never again will I destroy all living creatures." Then God blessed Noah and his sons and said, "Be fruitful and increase in number and again fill the earth." After God again promised never again to destroy all life on earth with a great flood God placed the rainbow in the sky as a sign of that promise. That is the story from God's Word the Bible.

Comfort the Heart:

1. Do you remember from the story why God brought a great flood upon the earth? Was God pleased with the wickedness and evil of the people in that day?
2. Did you notice why God was pleased with Noah? What did Noah do that was right and good?
3. How did God show his love for Noah and his family? (*God told Noah what was going to happen and what Noah must do to save his family and the animals.*)
4. Did Noah believe what God said was going to happen?
5. Did Noah obey what God told him to do?
6. After the flood was ended and Noah and his family and animals came out of the boat, what did Noah do to thank God?
7. Was God pleased with what Noah did?
8. What promise did God give Noah?
9. What command did God give to Noah and his sons?
10. Do you know that all people on earth today are descendants of Noah and his sons? What if Noah had disobeyed God and not built the boat? Do you think we would be here today?
11. Is obeying God important?
12. Do you believe that God also loves you and knows of your need? Do you believe that God is able to help you?
13. Noah's name means "comfort." Noah's father said that Noah would comfort his family in their labor and painful toil caused by the curse from the days of Adam and Eve.
14. God wants to comfort you and assure you of His love for you. Soon you will see in other stories how God helped people and comforted them in their need.

Remember the Blessing:

"As a father has compassion on his children, so the LORD has compassion on those who fear him..." (Psalm 103:13).

HOPE Stories

3. A Man God Blessed

Scripture Base: Genesis 11:27-12:8; 15:1-6; 18:1-14; 21:1-5; 22:1-18

Stir Their Thinking:

1. Do you know what it is like to be a stranger in a foreign land? Who would go with you? Who would help you?
2. What if someone told you to go to a foreign land and there you would receive a great blessing. Would you go?
3. This is a story about a man who received a blessing so that we might also receive a great blessing one day. Here is his story from God's Word.

Tell the Story:

A Man God Blessed

There was a man who was named Abram and his wife was Sarai. God had said to Abram, "Leave your country, your people and your father's household and go to the land I will show you. There I will make you a great nation and will bless you. I will make your name great, and you will be a blessing. I will bless those who bless you and curse those who curse you. And all peoples on earth will be blessed through you."

So Abram left his country and his people as God had told him. Abram was now seventy-five years old and his wife Sarai was sixty. They had no children. When they arrived in that land Abram walked through it and there God appeared to him and said, "To your offspring I am giving this land." So Abram built an altar and worshiped God and called on God's name.

Many years passed and still Abram and his wife Sarai had no son. Again God spoke to Abram saying, "I will give you a son fathered by you. Look up at the heavens and count the stars if you can. So shall your descendants be."

At another time God had again reassured Abram that he would indeed have a son and that God was giving that land to Abram and his descendants. Then God changed Abram's name to Abraham which means "the father of many nations." God also changed Sarai's name to Sarah which means "princess." God said, "Your wife Sarah will give birth to a son and you will call him Isaac. I will bless him, too, and his descendants. Abraham believed God and God counted Abraham as righteous.

Later three angels came to visit Abraham and Sarah. Abraham invited them to come and take rest and eat. After they had eaten, one of the angels said to Abraham, "Where is Sarah your wife? For I will return about this time next year and Sarah your wife will give birth to a son." When Sarah heard the angel's words she laughed and wondered how an old woman could have such a wonderful thing happen to her. The angel heard Sarah laugh and said to her, "Why did you laugh? Is anything too difficult for God to do?"

It happened just as God had promised for at the appointed time Sarah became with child and gave birth to a son and named him Isaac.

Later when Isaac was older God tested Abraham by asking Abraham to go to the place God would show him and there sacrifice his son Isaac. Early the next morning Abraham awoke and took two servants and his son Isaac. When they had cut enough wood for the sacrifice they set out for the place God would show Abraham. On the third day when Abraham saw the place, he told the servants to remain and he and Isaac would go worship and return again. Along the way Isaac asked his father, "Here is the wood and fire but where is the animal for the sacrifice?"

Abraham replied, "God will provide the sacrifice." At the appointed place Abraham built an altar and laid the wood upon it. Then he took his son Isaac and tied him and placed him on the altar and took his knife to kill his son. God called,

30

"Abraham! Abraham! Do not harm your son. For I know that you truly fear God because you have not kept your son from the sacrifice." God showed Abraham a sheep caught by its horns in a nearby thicket. Abraham offered the sheep as the sacrifice. God said, "I will surely bless you because you have done what I asked you to do. I will bless you and give you many descendants. And through one of your descendants all nations on earth will be blessed because you have obeyed me." And that is the end of the story from God's Word.

Comfort the Heart:

1. In the beginning what did God call Abram to do? Did Abram have any children then?
2. What things did God promise to do for Abram? Did you think that God would be able to fulfill those promises?
3. Did Abram believe God? Why did God count Abram righteous?
4. What was the meaning of Abraham's new name? Could it be telling Abraham that God was going to bless him?
5. God sent messengers to tell Abraham and Sarah what was going to happen in a year. What was it? Did God keep His promise?
6. How did God test Abraham? Did Abraham obey God?
7. Did Abraham have faith that God would keep his son Isaac alive? What did Abraham say to the servants? What did Abraham say to his son when Isaac asked about the animal for the sacrifice?
8. Did God provide the sacrifice as he promised?
9. Do you believe that we can trust God to do what He promises to do?
10. Do you know how God is going to bless you through Abraham and his son Isaac and Abraham's descendant?
11. Soon you will learn about that blessing and who brought it to us? You must believe God just as Abraham did.

Remember the Blessing:

"...being fully persuaded that God had power to do what he had promised" (Romans 4:21).

31

The HOPE Stories

4. God Comforted a Lonely Man

Scripture Base: Genesis 25: 21-34; 27:1-47; 28:10-22

Stir Their Thinking:

1. How is your relationship with your brothers or sisters?
2. How is your relationship with your father?
3. What might happen if you cheated your brother or deceived your father? What would you do?
4. Could God still bless you even if you were unworthy?
5. Here is a story about one of Abraham's descendants who dishonored his family and yet God chose to bless him.

Tell the Story:

God Comforted a Lonely Man

Before Jacob and his older twin brother were born God revealed to their mother that one day the older would serve the younger. The older son was the favorite of his father and the younger son Jacob the favorite of his mother. The older son Esau grew to be a man of the open fields who loved to hunt wild game. The younger son Jacob was a quiet man preferring to remain among the tents his family lived in.

One day when the older Esau was returning from hunting he had found nothing to kill. And he was very hungry. Jacob was cooking some stew. Esau demanded some of the stew because of his hunger. But Jacob would not give any to his brother until his brother Esau agreed to surrender his birthright to his father's inheritance. Then Jacob gave Esau the stew and Esau gave up his birthright.

Some time later their father, who was very old and thought he would die soon, decided to give Esau the older son his blessing. So the father called Esau to him and asked Esau to go hunt some wild game and prepare some tasty for food for his father. Then the father would give his blessing.

When the mother heard what was about to happen she quickly summoned Jacob and told him what to do in order for him to receive his father's blessing. So dressed in some of Esau's clothing and carrying some goat prepared as a tasty meal, Jacob went before his blind father. At first the father was not convinced that he was Esau the older. So he asked, "Are you really my son Esau?" Jacob replied, "Yes, I am." After his blind father had smelled the clothes of Esau he was finally convinced. And after eating the tasty food the father gave Jacob the blessing intended for Esau.

When Esau returned and learned what had happed he was very angry and thought to kill his brother. But the mother intervened and suggested that Jacob be sent away to find a wife from among their relatives in a distant place. Jacob's cleverness and desire for blessing had brought trouble for him. So Jacob left home to journey to his relatives.

When night came Jacob found a place to sleep and rested his head upon a stone and fell into a deep sleep. During the night God appeared to Jacob in a dream. In his dream Jacob saw a stairway reaching from earth to heaven. At the top was God, and angels were going up and down the stairway.

Then God spoke to Jacob saying: "I am the God of your father and your ancestors. I will give this land where you sleep to you and your descendants. You will have many descendants and all peoples on earth will be blessed through you. I will go with you and will watch over you wherever you go and will bring you safely back to this place. I will not leave you until I have done all that I promised you."

When Jacob awoke from sleep, he thought, "Surely God is in this place!" There Jacob set up a stone as a memorial and said, "If God will be with me and watch over me on this journey I am taking and will give me food to eat and clothes to wear so that I might return safely to my father's house, then he will be my God."

Jacob did find his relatives, was married and had twelve sons. Then God brought Jacob home again to meet his father and brother Esau who forgave him. That is the end of the Bible story.

Comfort the Heart:

1. What were you thinking about Jacob because of what he did to his brother and father?
2. If something like that happened in your home, would it cause bitter feelings with your family members?
3. Jacob's parents were able to prevent Esau from harming Jacob by sending Jacob away. What reason did they give for sending Jacob away?
4. If you were in Jacob's place, hated by your brother, having just dishonored your blind father by deceiving him, and now traveling alone to a distant place you had never visited—would you be lonely and afraid?
5. What did Jacob see when he fell into a deep sleep?
6. What did God say about Jacob's father and ancestors?
7. What promises did God make to Jacob?
8. Do you think these promises were comforting to Jacob?
9. Do you think that Jacob believed God would keep His promise? There are other stories that tell how God changed Jacob's heart because Jacob trusted God.
10. God had said to Abraham and then to Jacob's father and now to Jacob that God would one day bless all people through their descendant. You were included in that promise to one day receive a great blessing.
11. Do you believe that God is able to help you in all your troubles and needs?
12. I'm going to pray now that God will help you and your family with all that you need and that God will bless you.

Remember the Blessing:

"Taste and see that the LORD is good; blessed is the man who takes refuge in him" (Psalm 34:8).

Hope Stories

5. Blessed By God Even While In Prison

Scripture Base: Genesis 37:1-36; 39:1-41:44; 45:5; 50:20.

Stir Their Thinking:

1. Is anyone able to think of a place where one cannot be blessed by God?
2. Can good things happen to you, even in bad places? Here is a story about a man that God helped even while he was in prison.

Tell the Story:

Blessed by God Even While In Prison

Abraham's grandson Jacob had twelve sons. One of the younger sons named Joseph was his father's favorite because he was born in his father's old age. His father had made for Joseph a richly ornamented robe. Joseph had dreams that one day he would rule over his brothers and they would bow down to him. This made the brothers very jealous and angry. One day when Joseph was only a boy his father sent him out to meet his brothers who were with the sheep. When the brothers saw Joseph coming some wanted to kill Joseph. Instead they sold him as a slave to some merchants going down to Egypt.

There Joseph was employed to manage a wealthy Egyptian's home. When the wife of the owner wanted Joseph to sleep with her, he did not want to because it was wrong, so Joseph fled from the woman who kept part of Joseph's clothing. Then the woman gave a bad report to her husband about Joseph. The husband became very angry and had Joseph thrown into the prison where the king's prisoners were kept. But while Joseph was in prison God was with him and showed Joseph kindness and even granted Joseph favor in the eyes of the prison warden. The warden put Joseph in charge of all the other prisoners and he was responsible for all that was done there. The warden paid no attention to anything that was under Joseph's care, because God was with Joseph and gave him success in whatever he did.

Some time later two of the king's servants who were also in prison under Joseph's care had dreams that troubled them. When Joseph saw them the next morning they were dejected because no one could interpret their dreams. Joseph said that interpretation of dreams belongs to God. Each man told his dream to Joseph. It was good news for the man who served the king for he would be released in three days. But it was bad news for the king's baker who would be put to death.

Later when the king of Egypt had two troubling dreams he sent for Joseph who was brought out of prison to interpret the dreams. Joseph said that God would give the answer. The king was pleased with Joseph's interpretation and appointed Joseph to rule under the king to oversee food production before a coming famine.

Later when Joseph's brothers came to Egypt to buy food and they learned that Joseph was now a very powerful person under the king the brothers were afraid that Joseph would take revenge for what they did. But Joseph said, "Do not be angry with yourselves for selling me here, because it was to save lives that God sent me ahead of you...You intended to harm me, but God intended it for good..." So Joseph spoke kindly to his brothers and forgave them. That is the end of the story from God's Word.

Comfort the Heart:

1. What made Joseph so special to his father? What did Joseph's father do for him?
2. What did Joseph's brothers think about Joseph?
3. Because of their jealousy what did the brothers do to Joseph?

4. Even though Joseph was very young he was put in charge of a wealthy man's household. What problem did Joseph have with the man's wife?
5. Because of the wife's accusation what happened to Joseph?
6. Was God with Joseph while he was in prison? What happened that shows that God was blessing Joseph?
7. When the two men had dreams who did Joseph say was able to give the interpretation?
8. What good thing happened after it was known that Joseph with God's help could interpret dreams?
9. Do you think that God was still blessing Joseph?
10. What act of kindness did Joseph do toward his brothers?
11. Would you say that God had blessed Joseph's life?
12. Do you think that God can bless your life too, even when you face difficulties like Joseph?
13. Do you believe that God loves you just as he loved Joseph?
14. Have you ever asked God to help you, to bless you even in your difficulties?
15. I want to pray for you and your family now, asking God to demonstrate His love for you, to bless you and to help you.

Remember the Blessing:

"To you, O LORD, I lift up my soul; in you I trust, O my God. Do not let me be put to shame, nor let my enemies triumph over me. No one whose hope is in you will ever be put to shame..." (Psalm 25:1-3a).

"Joseph's master took him and put him in prison..." (Genesis 39:20).

Joseph's brother took him and put him in prison." (Genesis 39:20)

HOPE Stories

6. I Have Seen the Suffering of My People

Scripture Base: Exodus 1-4; 9:13-14; 14:21-22

Stir Their Thinking:

1. Who sees us when we suffer? Do you know who is watching you?
2. Is there anyone who cares when we suffer?
3. Who alone is powerful to help us when we suffer?

Tell the Story:

I Have Seen the Suffering of My People

During the days of Joseph the descendants of Abraham had gone to live in the land of Egypt during the great famine. Many years had passed and the family of Joseph and his brothers had grown into a nation of people. God was blessing them. But the king who had lived during the days of Joseph and who was favorably disposed toward Joseph's people had died and a new king arose who did not know Joseph or his people. In fact, the king and his people were now afraid that if an enemy nation should attack that the people who were Abraham's descendants might side with the enemy. So the king said, "We must deal shrewdly with these people or they will continue to increase in number."

So slave masters began to oppress the people with forced labor. The Egyptians worked the people ruthlessly and made their lives very bitter. But God was blessing the people and they continued to increase and spread throughout the land. The king then gave an order that all boy babies were to be killed at birth and later he ordered the babies to be thrown into the river to die.

A certain man and woman had a son born who was a fine baby. When the mother could no longer hide him at home she made a basket and placed the baby and the basket in the river. It happened that the king's daughter found the baby and gave him back to his own mother to nurse. Later the child came to grow up in the king's household. All was well until one day the man named Moses saw an overseer beating one of Moses' own people. In anger Moses killed the overseer and then had to flee out of the country.

After many years had passed Moses was now a shepherd tending sheep in a remote place. One day he happened to see a small tree that was burning and yet was not consumed by the fire. When Moses drew near to see the fire, God's voice spoke to him saying, "Moses, do not come any closer. Take off your shoes for you are standing on holy ground." Then God said, "I am the God of your own father and of your ancestor Abraham and his descendants." Moses hid his face because he was afraid.

Then God said, "I have indeed seen the misery of my people in Egypt. I have heard their crying out because of their slave drivers. I am concerned about their suffering. So I have come down to rescue them from the hand of those who oppress them. I am sending you to the king to bring my people out of their bondage. I will be with you"

But Moses said, "What if I go to my people and tell them what you said and they ask What is God's name? What shall I tell them? Then God revealed his holy name to Moses and instructed Moses on what he was to do before the king. Moses was still fearful, so God asked Moses to throw his shepherd's staff on the ground and it became a snake. When Moses picked it up it became his staff again.

As Moses returned to Egypt his older brother met him and together they went before the king of Egypt to tell him what God said. The king refused to listen even though Moses went before him many times. Each time the king refused God would send a plague upon the land. At last the king agreed to let the people go. Moses led the descendants of Abraham out of Egypt and through the sea that God had opened up for them. At last they were returning to their homeland. God had heard their cry and delivered them.

Comfort the Heart:

1. What caused the suffering of the descendants of Abraham? Had they done anything wrong to deserve harsh treatment and slavery?
2. Did God know of their suffering? Do you think God cared what happened to the people?
3. What plan did God have to deliver the people?
4. Even when the people suffered, did God continue to bless them? In what way?
5. Was God able to deliver the people from their suffering and bondage?
6. How did God help Moses to free the people?
7. Do you believe that God can help you in your need? Would you have faith to believe in the One that God sent to help all people in their greatest need? Soon you will hear about the One that God sent to be our help and deliverer.

Remember the Blessing:

"Cast your cares on the LORD and he will sustain you; he will never let the righteous fall" (Psalm 55:22).

"They made their lives bitter with hard labor in brick and mortar...in all their hard labor the Egyptians used them ruthlessly" (Exodus 1:14).

7. Delivered From a Hopeless Situation

Scripture Base: Genesis 13:17-14:31

Stir Their Thinking:

1. Have you ever felt that you were in a hopeless situation?
2. Has someone tried to help you who only made the situation worse?
3. Where would you turn for help in such a situation?

Tell the Story:

Delivered From a Hopeless Situation

After God performed many miraculous signs through Moses, the king of Egypt agreed to let the people go. However, God did not lead the people along the shorter way over the land. For God said, "If the people face war they might change their minds and decide to return to Egypt and slavery." So God led the people around by the desert way toward the Red Sea. When the people camped at the edge of the desert God went ahead of them in a cloud by day to guide them and as a pillar of fire at night to give them light. Neither the cloud by day nor the pillar of fire by night left its place before the people.

When God told Moses to have the people camp near the sea, the people began to wander around in confusion, hemmed in by the desert on one side and the sea on the other side. Then God said, "I will harden the king's heart and he will pursue the people to bring them back. But I will gain glory for myself through the king and all his army, so the Egyptians will know that I am God."

When the king heard that the people were camped near the sea he changed his mind and said, "What have we done? We have let the people go and have lost their services." So the king commanded that his army and all their war chariots be prepared to give chase.

As the king and his army came near where the people of Abraham were camped, the people saw the Egyptians marching toward them. The people cried out to Moses, "Was it because there were no graves in Egypt that you brought us to the desert to die? What have you done to us by bringing us out of Egypt? Why didn't you leave us alone? It would be better to serve the Egyptians than to die in the desert!"

Then Moses answered the people, "Do not be afraid. Stand firm and you will see how God will deliver you. God will fight for you."

Then God said to Moses, "Raise your staff and stretch out your hand over the sea to divide the water so the people can pass through the sea on dry ground." The angel of God who had been traveling in front of the people in the cloud and pillar of fire moved behind them and stood between the Egyptian army and the people. Throughout the night the cloud brought darkness to the Egyptians and light to the people of Abraham.

During the night God sent a strong east wind to drive back the water and open the sea to dry ground with a wall of water on either side. The descendants of Abraham went through the sea safely to the other side.

When the Egyptians pursued the people and were themselves in the midst of the sea, God threw the Egyptian army into confusion, causing the wheels of their chariots to fall off. Then God said to Moses, "Stretch out your hand over the sea so the waters may flow back and cover the Egyptians. When Moses obeyed, the waters covered the fleeing Egyptians so that the entire army was drowned.

On that day God saved the people from the hands of the Egyptians and delivered them safely out of Egypt. Because of this, the people feared God and put their trust in God and in Moses who was God's servant. That is the story from God's Word.

Comfort the Heart:

1. What purpose do you think God had by bringing the people into the desert to camp near the sea?
2. Do you think that God knew the king would change his mind and come after the people?
3. How did God lead the people by day and night?
4. When the Egyptians came and the people saw them, what did the people say would be better to do? Do you think that was a wise choice?
5. How did God stop the Egyptians from coming any closer to the people?
6. What did God tell Moses to do? Did Moses obey God?
7. What happened when Moses obeyed God?
8. Did the people cross through the water or on dry ground?
9. When the Egyptians tried to follow through the sea what did God tell Moses to do?
10. Who was more powerful—the king of Egypt and his army or God and his servant Moses?
11. When the people saw what happened and how God saved them, they feared God and trusted God and Moses. If God helps you in your need would you fear Him and trust God to provide your needs?

Remember the Blessing:

"The LORD is my strength and my song; he has become my salvation. He is my God and I will praise him...I will exalt him" (Exodus 15:2).

8. God Provided Water for Thirsty People

Scripture Base: Exodus 15:22-27; 17:1-6

Stir Their Thinking:

1. Have you ever been really thirsty?
2. What if there were no water to be found for drinking?
3. Who could help you to find water for your thirst?
4. Here is the story of a people who needed water and how God provided it.

Tell the Story:

God Provided Water for Thirsty People

God helped Moses to lead the descendants of Abraham out of the land of Egypt. They traveled through the desert without finding water. Finally the people came to a place where the water was bitter and they could not drink it. The people began to grumble against Moses asking, "What are we to drink?"

Moses cried out to God on account of the people. Then God showed Moses a piece of wood. Moses took the wood and threw it into the water and the water became sweet. Later God led the people to a place where there were twelve springs of water and many palm trees. The people camped there.

When God led the people farther through the desert there was again no water to drink. The people quarreled with Moses saying, "Give us water to drink."

Moses replied, "Why do you quarrel with me? Why do you put God to the test?"

49

But the people were very thirsty for water there. So they said, "Why did you bring us up out of Egypt to make us and our children and livestock die of thirst?"

Again Moses asked God, "What am I to do? These people are ready to stone me!"

Then God said, "Walk on ahead of the people. Take with you some of the elders among the people. And take in your hand your staff. I will go and stand before you by a certain rock. Take your staff and strike the rock and water will come out for the people to drink. Moses did this in the sight of all the people.

So God split the rocks in the desert and gave the people water as abundant as the seas; he brought streams of water out and made it flow down like a river (Psalm 78:15-16).

That is the end of the story from God's Word.

Comfort the Heart:

1. The people have lived as slaves while in Egypt, now God has delivered them in a powerful way through the sea. Now can God provide water for the people to drink as they travel?
2. When the people came to water that was bitter, who did they complain to? What did Moses do?
3. Briefly tell the Creation story to show that God made the earth and the seas. In that story it reminds us that God is the Creator of all.
4. God revealed to Moses what he must do to make the water safe to drink. Did Moses use the wood that God showed him?
5. Again where there was no water did the people turn to God for water or did they complain against their leader Moses?
6. What did Moses do when the people demanded water?
7. Was God concerned about the people and their livestock?
8. Did God help Moses to provide the needed water?

9. Do you think there was plenty of water to satisfy all the thirsty people and their livestock?
10. When you are thirsty and need good water to drink, do you believe that God cares about you? Do you believe that God can provide water for your thirst?
11. There is another thirst that you will hear about later. It is a thirst in our inner spirit. A thirst to satisfy our deepest need. You will hear another story about how God satisfied the thirst of a woman who came to a well to draw water to drink and was instead given living water so she would never thirst again.

Remember the Blessing:

"For *God* satisfies the thirsty and fills the hungry with good things" (Psalm 107:9).

"...for they drank from the spiritual rock that accompanied them, and that rock was Christ" (1 Corinthians 10:4).

9. God Provided Food for Hungry People

Scripture Base: Exodus 16:3-35; Psalm 78:23-29

Stir Their Thinking:

1. When our food is gone and we are hungry what we do?
2. Who can provide our food when we are hungry?
3. If you are really hungry would you eat whatever is provided for you, even if it is different from what you like to eat? Here's the story of food for hungry people.

Tell the Story:

God Provided Food for Hungry People

God continued to lead the descendants of Abraham in their journey to a promised land that flowed with milk and honey. But soon after leaving Egypt their food was gone and now the people were hungry. So the people complained to Moses saying, "If only we had died by God's hand in Egypt! There we sat around pots of meat and ate all the food we wanted. But you have brought us out into this desert to starve all the people to death."

Then God said to Moses, "I will rain down bread from heaven for you. The people are to go out each day and gather enough for that day. On the sixth day they are to gather enough for two days. I will test the people to see if they follow my instructions."

So Moses said to all the people, "In the evening you will know that it was God who brought you out of Egypt, and in the morning you will see God's glory because He has heard your grumbling against him. You will know that it is God who gives you meat to eat in the evening and all the bread you want in the morning."

In the morning there appeared on the ground flakes of food. So the people did as they were told; some gathered much and some gathered little. When they measured it, those who gathered much did not have too much, and those who gathered little did not have too little. Each one gathered as much as they needed. When the sun grew hot the food melted away. On the sixth day the people gathered twice as much for that day and the next day. God instructed the people to bake or boil the food to eat on the seventh day. Some did not obey God's command and gathered too much food which spoiled by the next day. And on the sixth day some gathered too little and found there was no food on the seventh day for on that day the people were to rest.

In addition God sent quails each evening which the people caught and cooked for their meat. In this way God provided meat each evening and bread each morning so the people would know it was God who fed them. That is the end of the story from God's Word.

Comfort the Heart:

1. What complaint did the people make against Moses and God?
2. Was God concerned about their hunger?
3. Did the people trust God to provide their food?
4. What plan did God have for providing food? What instruction did God give the people?
5. Did the people follow God's instruction? What happened when they disobeyed?
6. How did God provide meat for the people?
7. Does God know about your hunger and that of your people?
8. Do you believe that God can help to provide food?
9. Would you follow God's instruction about food and give God the glory for providing it?
10. Later we will have a story about an even more wonderful food, and whoever eats it will never hunger.

Remember the Blessing:

"But here is bread that comes down from heaven, which a man may eat and not die" (John 6:50).

10. God Provided Healing From Poisonous Snakes

Scripture Base: Numbers 21:4-9

Stir Their Thinking:

1. Have you ever grumbled because you were unhappy?
2. What if your grumbling led to serious consequences for you and your people?
3. Would you do whatever was necessary to escape the consequences or punishment for your grumbling?

Tell the Story:

God Provided Healing From Poisonous Snakes

God continued to lead Abraham's descendants from Egypt where they had served as slaves to a good land that God had promised the people. Along the journey the people began to grow impatient and to complain. They spoke against Moses and against God saying, "Why have you brought us out of Egypt only to die in the desert? There is no bread! There is no water! And we detest this miserable food that God is providing us!"

Then God sent poisonous snakes among the people. The snakes bit the people and many of the people died. When this happened the people came to Moses and confessed: "We sinned when we spoke against you and against God. Pray for us that God will take the snakes away from us." So Moses prayed for the people.

God said to Moses, "Make a snake and put it up on a pole so that anyone who is bitten by a snake may look at the snake on the pole." So Moses did as God commanded and made a bronze snake and put it up on a pole so that everyone could see it. Then whenever anyone was bitten by a poisonous snake and looked at the bronze snake they lived. That ends the story from God's Word.

Comfort the Heart:

1. Why were the people grumbling? Do you think this was a good thing to do? God had provided their water and their food.
2. What happened because of their grumbling? Does this teach us anything about complaining against God's provision for us?
3. Did God know about the people's grumbling?
4. Even though God judged the people's grumbling as wrong, do you think that God still loved the people?
5. How did God express his love for the people?
6. What did God require of the people in order to be healed after they had grumbled and then been bitten by a poisonous snake?
7. What happened if the people, after they were bitten, happened to disobey what God said they must do?
8. The people had to believe God and obey God in order to be healed. Do you believe that God can deliver you from your troubles?
9. Would you obey what God has asked us to do in order to be healed of our greatest sickness?

Remember the Blessing:

"He (God) forgives all my sins and heals all my diseases; he redeems my life from the pit and crowns me with love and compassion" (Psalm 103:3-4).

11. Hope for a Fearful Woman
And Her Family

Scripture Base: Joshua 2:1-21; 6:22-25

Stir Their Thinking:

1. What would you be willing to do to save your life and that of your family?
2. Here is a story about a woman who heard terrifying reports about what the God of Abraham's people did to the Egyptians. She had to decide what to do after hearing these reports. Listen to the story to see what instructions were given to the woman and what she must do in order to save herself and her family.

Tell the Story:

Hope for a Fearful Woman
And Her Family

As God led the people of Abraham to the land of promise the people had to defeat a wicked people already living in that land. Two spies were chosen to go and spy out one of their cities which had strong walls to protect it. While in the city, the men entered into the house of a woman who was a prostitute named Rahab. The king of the city learned about the two spies and sent a message to the woman Rahab to bring out the two men as enemies. But Rahab had taken the two men and hidden them.

So she said, "Yes, the men came to me, but I did not know where they came from. When evening came and it was time to close the city gate, the men left. I don't know which way they went." Rahab had taken the two men up to the roof of her house and hidden them under the stalks of reeds she had laid out to dry on the roof.

Before the two men lay down to sleep for the night Rahab came to them and said, "I know that the LORD God has given this land to you. A great fear of your people has fallen upon all of us, for all who live in this country are melting in fear. We have heard how your God dried up the water of the Red Sea for you when you came out of Egypt. Also we heard what happened to the two kings who opposed you and were destroyed. When we heard of it, our hearts and courage failed. The LORD your God is God in heaven above and on earth below."

Then the woman begged the two men saying, "Swear to me that you will show kindness to me and my family, because I have shown kindness to you. Give me a sure sign that you will spare the lives of my father and mother, my brothers and sisters, and all who belong to them—that you will save us from death."

"Our lives for your lives!" the two men assured her. "If you don't tell what we are doing we will treat you kindly and faithfully when your city is destroyed and our God gives us this land." So Rahab let the two men who were spies down by a rope from a window because her house was on the city wall. The men also said to Rahab, "You must tie a red cord in your window and bring all your family members into your house when the time comes. If anyone goes outside their blood will be on their own head." So Rahab agreed to the terms and the men departed and later made their report to their own people.

When time came for the descendants of Abraham with God's help to destroy the city, the same two men were sent to save Rahab and her family. So they went to the house with the red cord in the window and brought out Rahab, her father and mother and brothers and all who belonged to her. The two men brought out Rahab's entire family and put them in a safe place. Then the city was destroyed and all who lived in it. But Rahab and her family continued to live among Abraham's people.

After many generations had passed one of Rahab's descendants would come to save his people from their sins and a coming judgment, and also to save us from destruction because of our sins. That is the end of the story from God's Word.

Comfort the Heart:

1. You've heard the story about Rahab. Do you think it was just chance that the two men who were spies happened to go to her house?
2. What did Rahab know about Abraham's people and their God? Did she believe the reports about what God had done in Egypt and to the two kings?
3. How do you feel about Rahab's cleverness in sending her own king's messengers away and hiding the two spies?
4. What did Rahab say about her own people after they heard the reports about God?
5. What plan did Rahab have to save her life and that of her family?
6. Did the two spies agree to Rahab's request?
7. How did Rahab help the two spies to escape?
8. What sign to mark Rahab's house did the two spies ask for?
9. What must Rahab and her entire family do in order to be safe?
10. Did the two spies keep their word to rescue Rahab and her family?
11. Can we say that Rahab feared God, believed that the two spies could her save her family, and then obeyed what they said she must do?
12. If we hear reports of a coming destruction and are told what to do to save ourselves and our families, would we be willing to do it?

Remember the Blessing:

"...God does not show favoritism but accepts men from every nation who fear him and do what is right" (Acts 10:34b-35).

12. A Husband and Son for a Faithful Widow

Scripture Base: Ruth 1-4

Stir Their Thinking:

1. Is anyone listening to this story who is a widow? If so, tell about your sorrow in losing your husband?
2. Is it your custom to remain with the dead husband's mother? Can you go back to your own family?
3. What would be the greatest blessing you could have as a widow? Here is the story of a young woman whose husband died leaving her childless. But she made a wise choice and in turn received a great blessing.

Tell the Story:

A Husband and Son for a Faithful Widow

There was a certain man, a descendant of Abraham, who with his wife and two sons went to a foreign land to find food during a famine. There the two sons married local women. In time the father of the sons died leaving the wife Naomi a widow. The two sons also died before any children were born. One of the girls decided to return to her own people. The other girl named Ruth said to her mother-in-law Naomi, "Don't urge me to leave you or to turn back from you. Where you go I will go, and where you stay I will stay. Your people will be my people, and your God my God. Where you die, I will die, and there I will be buried. May your God deal with me severely if anything but death separates you and me." So Naomi stopped urging Ruth to return home.

Naomi decided to return to her own country and people. When she arrived the people were glad to see her saying, "Can this be Naomi?"

"Don't call me Naomi," she said, "instead call me Mara, or bitter, because my life has become very bitter." And so she blamed God for what happened to her.

Now the barley harvest was just beginning. Ruth said, "Let me go to the fields and glean the grain the harvesters have dropped." It happened that Ruth went to the fields of a relative of Naomi's dead husband.

When the man Boaz saw Ruth he asked, "Whose young woman is that?" So he learned that she was a foreign woman of good character who had married one of Naomi's sons. When Boaz saw how Ruth had worked hard he said to her, "Don't go to another field. Stay here with my servant girls. I have told the men not to touch you." When Ruth returned to Naomi she brought the grain she gathered and good news of what had happened.

When Naomi heard where Ruth had worked and about Boaz, she said, "God has not stopped showing his kindness to me." So Naomi explained to Ruth that Boaz was a relative. One day later Naomi said, "I should try to find a home for you where you will be provided for." So she told Ruth that she should bathe and put on perfume and fresh clothes and go down to the threshing floor and hide. When the men and Boaz lay down to sleep, then Ruth was to go and uncover Boaz' feet. Then Naomi added, "Boaz will know what to do."

During the night Ruth did as Naomi told her and lay down at the feet of Boaz. When he awoke Boaz found Ruth and said, "May God bless you my daughter, this is a great kindness for you have not gone after the younger men." When morning came Boaz went to the town gate and offered to redeem the land belonging to his dead relative. Another man had a closer claim but declined to redeem the land. So Boaz redeemed the land and with it came the widow Ruth whom he married.

God enabled Ruth to conceive and she bore a son. Naomi took the son and held him in her lap and cared for him. The women were saying, "Naomi has a son! Praise God for he has provided a kinsman redeemer. For your daughter-in-law who loves you and who is better to you than seven sons, has given birth." And that son of Boaz and Ruth became an ancestor of the Coming One who was going to bless not only his own people, but all peoples in the world.

That is the story from God's Word.

Comfort the Heart:

1. What bad thing happened to Naomi and her daughters-in-law?
2. What did one of the girls decide to do?
3. What did Naomi want Ruth to do?
4. What was Ruth's decision? How did she show her love for Naomi?
5. Do you think it was Ruth's good luck where she went to glean barley? Or was it the kindness of God because of Ruth's faithful commitment to Naomi?
6. How did Boaz show his kindness to Ruth?
7. What was Naomi's plan to help Ruth find a husband?
8. Did Naomi's plan work?
9. In the story who really helped Ruth to conceive and have a son?
10. What did the women have to say about Naomi and Ruth's son?
11. Do you think Naomi was now happy again?
12. You might be interested to know that the town where Naomi and Ruth and Boaz lived was going to be the birthplace of the Coming One who will bless all peoples.

Remember the Blessing:

"I will tell of the kindnesses of the LORD, the deeds for which he is to be praised, according to all the LORD has done for us—" (Isaiah 63:7a).

HOPE Stories

13. The End of Famine for a Hopeless Widow

Scripture Base: 1 Kings 17:1-16

Stir Their Thinking:

1. What would you do if you were preparing to eat the very last food in your house and a stranger asks you to share it with him?
2. Many of our stories have been about the descendants of Abraham that God blessed. Here is another story about a foreign woman, a widow, who was poor and about to starve unless someone helped her to have food.

Tell the Story:

The End of Famine for a Hopeless Widow

The king of the land had married a foreign princess who brought with her a religion that greatly offended God. Because of this God had sent a prophet to proclaim, "As the LORD, the God of Abraham's people lives, whom I serve, there will be neither dew nor rain in the next few years, except at my word." So without any rain the crops soon died from the drought and a famine was upon the land.

First God had sent the prophet to hide in a certain place where he could drink from a small stream and be fed by ravens who brought him bread and meat in the morning and meat in the evening. The prophet stayed there for a time but soon even the stream dried up because there had been no rain in the land. Then God said, "Go at once to a certain place in a neighboring country and stay there. I have commanded a widow in that place to supply you with food."

When the prophet came to the town gate, a widow was there gathering sticks. The prophet called to her and asked, "Would you bring me a little water in a jar so I may drink?"

As the widow was going to get the water, the prophet called to her, "And please bring me a piece of bread."

"As surely as the LORD your God lives," the widow replied, "I don't have any bread—only a handful of flour in a jar and a little oil in a jug. I am gathering a few sticks to take home and make a meal for myself and my son, that we may eat it—and die."

The prophet said, "Don't be afraid. Go home and do as you have said. But first, make a small cake of bread for me from what you have and bring it to me. Then make something for yourself and your son. For this is what God says: 'The jar of flour will not be used up and the jug of oil will not run dry until God gives rain on the land.'"

The widow went to her house and did as the prophet told her. So there was food every day for the prophet and for the woman and for her family. The jar of flour was not used up and the jug of oil did not run dry, in keeping with the word of God spoken by the prophet. That is the story from God's Word.

Comfort the Heart:

1. How did God show his concern for the prophet during the drought?
2. When the stream dried up, who did God say would now feed the prophet?
3. What was the woman doing when the prophet saw her and spoke to her?
4. What did the prophet ask the woman to do for him?
5. What promise did the prophet make to the woman?
6. Did the woman obey what the prophet said to do?
7. Did the prophet's words come true?
8. Who was the promise really from—the prophet or God?
9. If you had been the woman, would you have obeyed the words of the prophet?
10. Is God able to provide food for you and your family?

Remember the Blessing:

"The eyes of all look to you, and you give them their food at the proper time" (Psalm 145:15).

HOPE Stories

14. God Sent Rain to End the Drought

Scripture Base: 1 Kings 17:1; 18:1-45

Stir Their Thinking:

1. Sometimes bad things happen to us because of what we do or our leaders do. Can you think of any bad thing that has happened because of you or what your leaders have done?
2. Some of the descendants of Abraham had turned away from worshiping the true God of this world. Because of this God sent a drought to turn their hearts back to him.

Tell the Story:

God Sent Rain to End the Drought

Because the king and many people were worshiping a false god and not the true God there was now a drought throughout the land. God spoke through the prophet Elijah who said: "There will be neither dew nor rain for the next few years except at my command." This was God's judgment upon the king and the people because of their sin.

In the third year of the drought God said to Elijah, "Go show yourself to the king and I will send rain upon the land." Because of the drought there was a severe famine in the land. The king was searching for grass for his animals to eat. When Elijah saw the king he said, "You have made trouble for all the people because you abandoned God's commands and have followed false gods. Now go and call all the people and the false prophets and have them meet me on the mountain." So the king did as Elijah said.

When the people assembled Elijah said to them, "How long will you waver between two opinions? If the LORD is God,

67

follow him. If the god you now worship is the true God, then follow him." But the people said nothing.

Then Elijah said to the people, "Get two animals for the sacrifices. Choose one for yourselves and prepare an altar with wood and place the animal on the altar. But set no fire to it. I will do the same. Then have your prophets call on the name of your god and I will call on the name of the LORD. The god who answers by fire—he is the true God."

The false prophets prepared their altar and then began to chant and dance as they prayed. But no fire came. Elijah mocked them saying, "Call louder, your god may be away traveling or sleeping." So the false prophets danced harder, called louder and even cut themselves. But there was no fire.

The Elijah called the people to himself. He repaired the altar of God which had fallen into ruins. After he placed the wood and animal on the altar, Elijah commanded, "Fill four large jars with water and pour it on the altar." He did this three times so that water ran down and even filled the trench about the altar.

Then at the time of sacrifice Elijah began to pray: "O LORD answer me so these people will know that you are turning their hearts back again to you." Then God sent fire that fell and burned up the sacrifice, the altar and even licked up the water on the ground.

When the people saw this they fell on their faces and cried, "The LORD—he is God! The LORD—he is God!"

After the false prophets had been put to death Elijah said to the king, "Go, eat and drink, for there is the sound of heavy rain." Seven times Elijah sent his servant to look toward the sea. The seventh time the servant reported that a small cloud was rising from the sea. Soon the sky grew black with clouds, the wind rose, and a heavy rain began to fall. The drought was ended and the people had turned back to the true God. That ends the story from God's Word.

Comfort the Heart:

1. Why had God sent a drought on the land?
2. If we do not honor God properly, could it be that trouble will come our way?
3. What did Elijah call the people to do?
4. Were the false prophets successful in calling for fire to burn their sacrifice? Why do you think they failed?
5. What unusual thing did Elijah command to be done to his sacrifice?
6. When Elijah began to pray what happened? What did the fire consume?
7. What did the people do when they saw the fire and what happened?
8. What did the people say?
9. Was God pleased with the people when they turned their hearts back to him?
10. Did Elijah believe that rain was coming?
11. Did the rain come just as Elijah said it would?
12. Where is your heart turned? Do you need to turn your heart toward the true God?
13. The people had suffered for three years because they failed to honor the true God. God used the drought to bring the people before him and the sacrifice to demonstrate that He alone is the true God in heaven and on earth.

Remember the Blessing:

"If you follow my decrees and are careful to obey my commands, I will send you rain in its season, and the ground will yield its crops and the trees of the field their fruit" (Leviticus 26:3-4).

HOPE Stories

15. Hope for a Proud Leper

Scripture Base: 2 Kings 5:1-19

Stir Their Thinking:

1. Long ago leprosy was a disease that caused people to become outcasts and considered unclean.
2. Do you know anyone who has leprosy?
3. What would a person be willing to do to be healed and considered clean again? Here is the story of a man who heard about a God who could heal him.

Tell the Story:

Hope for a Proud Leper

Naaman was commander of his king's army. He was a great man in the sight of his king and a valiant soldier, but he was a leper. Naaman's wife had a young servant girl who had been taken captive from among the descendants of Abraham. The servant girl said to her mistress, "If only my master would see the prophet who lives in my country—he could cure my master of his leprosy." So Naaman went to the king and told him what the servant girl had said. The king wrote a letter of introduction for Naaman who departed, taking with him a large sum of money and clothing to pay for being cured of leprosy.

First Naaman went to the king of the country his servant girl was from. The king was greatly distressed that Naaman was asking him how to be cured of leprosy. The king thought that Naaman was trying to pick a quarrel with him.

Then the prophet of God learned of Naaman's visit and sent this message, "Have Naaman come to me and then he will know there is a prophet of God in this country." So Naaman

71

went with all his horses and chariots and stopped at the prophet's house.

The prophet did not come out to meet Naaman but instead sent his servant with this message, "Go wash yourself seven times in the nearby river, and your flesh will be restored and you will be made clean again."

When Naaman saw that the prophet did not come out to meet him and call on the name of his God and place his hand over the leprosy and cure him, he was angry. Naaman said, "Are not the rivers of my own country better than the rivers here? Couldn't I wash in my own rivers and be made clean" So Naaman turned and went away in a rage.

Naaman's servants said to him, "My father, if the prophet told you to do some great thing, wouldn't you have done it? Why don't you do what the prophet tells you—to wash and be made clean?" So Naaman went to the river and bathed seven times as the prophet of God said. Naaman's flesh was restored and became like that of a young boy.

Then Naaman and all his servants went back to the prophet of God and said, "Now I know there is no God in all the world except among your people. Please accept a gift from me."

But the prophet of God replied, "As surely as the LORD lives, whom I serve, I will not accept a thing." And even though Naaman urged him, the prophet refused to accept a gift. "Go in peace," the prophet of God said. And so Naaman returned to his own country cleansed of his leprosy. That is the end of the story from God's Word.

Comfort the Heart:

1. Who told where Naaman might be made clean?
2. What did Naaman expect the prophet of God to do?
3. What did the prophet tell Naaman to do to be healed?
4. Was Naaman glad or angry to learn what he must do?
5. What happened when Naaman obeyed the prophet?
6. Who really healed Naaman—the prophet or God?

Remember the Blessing:

"Heal me, O LORD, and I will be healed; save me and I will be saved, for you are the one I praise" (Jeremiah 17:14).

16. A Faithful Man Is Delivered From Death

Scripture Base: Daniel 6:1-26

Stir Their Thinking:

1. Do you know anyone who is persecuted or threatened because of their worship of the true God?
2. If you were threatened with harm or death, would your faith be strong to trust in God in all circumstances?
3. Here is the story about a man who was falsely accused because he was faithful to his living God.

Tell the Story:

A Faithful Man Is Delivered From Death

There was a man named Daniel who was taken into exile to a foreign country while he was still a young man. There God blessed Daniel and because of his faithfulness Daniel was given a high position as an administrator in the government of that kingdom.

Daniel had so distinguished himself that the king planned to set Daniel over the whole kingdom. At this the other administrators and leaders tried to find grounds for charges against Daniel in his government work. But they were unable to do so, for they could find no corruption in Daniel because he was trustworthy. Finally these men said, "We will never find any basis for charges against this man Daniel unless it has something to do with the law of his God."

So the jealous administrators went to the king and said, "O King, live forever! All the administrators are agreed that the king should issue a decree that anyone who prays to any god or man in the next month shall be thrown into the lions' den." So the king put the decree into writing.

73

When Daniel heard about the decree, he went home to his upstairs window which opened toward his home country. Three times a day Daniel bowed on his knees and prayed, giving thanks to his God, just as he had always done. Then the jealous administrators saw Daniel praying and asking God for help. So the administrators went to the king and asked, "Didn't you publish a decree that during the next month anyone who prays to any god or man, except to you, would be thrown into the lions' den?"

The king replied, "The decree stands and cannot be undone."

Then the administrators said to the king, "The man Daniel pays no attention to you, O King, or to the decree you put into writing. He still prays to his God three times a day." When the king heard this, he was greatly distressed and was determined to rescue Daniel and struggled until sundown to save Daniel. Then the administrators reminded the king that all decrees must be enforced. So the king gave the order, and they brought Daniel and threw him into the lions' den.

The king said to Daniel, "May your God, whom you serve continually, rescue you." Then a stone cover was placed over the opening to the den and the king sealed it so that Daniel could not be removed. Then the king returned to his palace and spent the night without eating or sleeping. At the first light of day the king hurried to the lions' den and called to Daniel with an anguished voice, "Daniel, servant of the living God, has your God, whom you serve faithfully, been able to rescue you from the lions?"

Daniel answered, "O king, live forever! My God sent his angel, and he shut the mouths of the lions. They have not hurt me, because I was found innocent in God's sight. What have I done to offend you, O king?"

The king was overjoyed and gave orders to lift Daniel out of the den. There was no wound found on Daniel because he had trusted in his God. At the king's command, those men who had falsely accused Daniel were brought and thrown into the lions' den where the lions overpowered them. Then the king issued a new decree saying: "People must fear and reverence the God of Daniel. For he is the living God and he endures forever." That is the end of the story from the Bible.

Comfort the Heart:

1. Was Daniel a good administrator? What had the king planned to do for Daniel?
2. Why do you think the other administrators were jealous toward Daniel?
3. What sly plan did the jealous administrators have to trap Daniel and have him killed?
4. In the beginning did their plan work?
5. When Daniel learned about the king's decree did he stop praying to his God?
6. What did the jealous administrators do when they saw Daniel praying according to his custom?
7. Did the king want to see Daniel die? What did the king do that night after Daniel was thrown into the lions' den?
8. What did the king ask Daniel the next morning?
9. How did God rescue Daniel during the night?
10. How did the king punish the jealous administrators?
11. What new decree did the king issue about Daniel's God?
12. Would you be bold to face death like Daniel because of your faith in the living God?
13. What message of hope have you learned from this story?
14. Soon there will be the story of what God has done to rescue us from the judgment of sin. The Bible says: "The LORD is not slow in keeping his promise...He is patient with you, not wanting anyone to perish, but everyone to come to repentance" (2 Peter 6:9).

Remember the Blessing:

"For you, O LORD, have delivered my soul from death, my eyes from tears, my feet from stumbling, that I may walk before the LORD in the land of the living..." (Psalm 116:8-9).

HOPE Stories

17. Someone to Suffer In Our Place

Scripture Base: Isaiah 53:1-12

Stir Their Thinking:

1. Many people have stories of how an innocent person took the punishment for a guilty person, usually a member of their own family. Do you know a story like this among your own people?
2. What if you were judged guilty of some wrongdoing and were to be punished—then someone stepped forward and offered to take your punishment? Here is the prophecy about a story in which that very thing happened. Later we will have the story which fulfills this prophecy.

Tell the Story:

Someone to Suffer In Our Place

Do you remember from the story of Abraham and Isaac that Isaac asked his father, "Where is the lamb for the sacrifice?" Abraham answered, "God will provide the lamb." That sacrificial lamb is actually a person who was to come one day.

One of the great prophets among Abraham's descendants told this prophecy from God. One day a person would come who had no beauty or majesty that would attract us to him. In fact, he was to be rejected and despised by his own people, a man of sorrows who was familiar with suffering and those who suffer.

He would be like one that men hide their faces from, and people would not realize who he was. But this person would take our sickness and weakness and carry our sorrows. We would see him struck by God and afflicted by men.

77

His hands and feet and side would be pierced for our wrongdoing and crushed for our sins (Psalm 22:16; Zechariah 12:10). The very punishment that brings us peace would be upon him. It would be by his wounds that we ourselves are healed. We are all like sheep that have gone astray, each wandering his own way; and the LORD has laid upon this one to suffer for the sin of all.

This suffering one was oppressed and afflicted, yet he did not open his mouth in protest. For he was like a sheep being led to slaughter, and as a sheep before her shearers is silent, he did not open his mouth.

By oppression and judgment he was taken away and put to death; for the sins of the people he was put to death. He died among the wicked and was buried in a grave with the rich, even though he had done no violence and there was no deceit in his mouth.

It was God's will to crush him and cause him to suffer and make his life a guilt offering. But his body will not see decay in the grave (Psalm 16:10). After the suffering of his soul he will again see the light of life and be satisfied. By his righteous knowledge this one who suffered will justify many before God and bear their sins.

God will give him a place of high honor because he poured out his life unto death, being numbered among those who are transgressors of a holy God. This Suffering One not only bore the sin of many but he makes intercession for those who sin.

Other prophets said the coming One would be born of a virgin and called him Emmanuel or "God with man". He would be born in a town called Bethlehem. God would call him his own Son (Psalm 2:7). He would be betrayed by one who shared his bread (Psalm 41:9), falsely accused (Psalm 27:12), beaten and mocked (Isaiah 50:6; Psalm 22:6). People would gamble for his clothing (Psalm 22:18), yet he would forgive those who put him to death (Luke 23:34).

Before this would happen another prophet would come proclaiming to the people to repent of their sins and prepare the way for the coming of the LORD. That same prophet exclaimed upon seeing this coming One: "Behold the Lamb of God who takes away the sin of the world" (John 1:29)!

Comfort the Heart:

1. Did you know this prophecy includes you, for your sins were included in His suffering?
2. A prophet wrote: "Since the children (people like us) have flesh and blood, he too shared in their humanity..." (Hebrews 2:14a). "For this reason he had to be made like his brothers in every way, in order that he might become a merciful and faithful high priest serving God. And that he might make atonement for the sins of the people" (Hebrews 2:17). He suffered so that he might in turn help those who suffer.
3. There was a great religious and military leader in a certain country by the name of Shamyl, who died in 1871. Bribery was so widespread in his kingdom that he made a penalty of one hundred lashes for anyone caught taking or giving a bribe. One day a culprit was brought before Shamyl. He turned pale. It was his own mother! What would he do? Lightly forgive? He was too just for that. Would he do nothing to save her? He was too loving for that. So he ordered the lash.

   First came one blow—then 2, 3, 4, 5. Then suddenly Shamyl cried out, "Halt!" He knelt in his mother's place and took the remaining 95 lashes. Some exclaimed, "How just!" Others said, "How loving!" Actually, it was both. Shamyl kept the righteous law, but he saved his mother. Two things come together — justice and mercy, law and love. From this the followers of Shamyl caught a vision of how deeply just their master was. He would not change his righteous laws, and yet he saved the guilty.
4. This suffering One in the prophecy has taken your punishment for your wrongdoing for God loves you.

Remember the Blessing:

"For he bore the sin of many, and made intercession for the transgressors" (Isaiah 53:12b).

HOPE Stories

18. A Savior and a Light

Scripture Base: Matthew 1:18-25; 2:1-2, 11; Luke 1:26-38, 2:4-40

Stir Their Thinking:

1. If a messenger came to tell you of a wonderful thing that was going to happen to you, what would you say? Would you believe the messenger?
2. How do you think God might fulfill his promise to send a special person to suffer for our sins? Who would his mother be?
3. What do you think God might say to announce the birth of this child? Who would be the first to hear the good news? What would people say about the child? Listen to the story and see what happened.

Tell the Story:

A Savior and a Light

The time came when God sent an angel to a young woman named Mary to announce that she was going to bear a son. The angel said, "Do not be afraid, Mary, you have found favor with God. You will give birth to a son and are to name him 'Jesus'. He will be called Son of the Most High God. For God's Holy Spirit will come upon you so that the holy one to be born will be called the Son of God."

Mary said, "I am the Lord's servant. May it happen as you have said." Now Mary was promised in marriage to a man named Joseph, but they had not yet come together as man and wife. But Joseph found that Mary was now going to have a child so Joseph wanted to quietly put her away. The angel came in a dream to tell Joseph, "Do not be afraid to take Mary as your wife." She was to give birth to a son and he was to be named Jesus. Joseph did what the angel

81

commanded but had no union with Mary his wife until after the child was born.

Joseph took his wife Mary with him to a town called Bethlehem to register for a census. While there the time came for Mary to deliver her son. On the hillside outside of the town there were shepherds keeping watch over their flocks of sheep. An angel appeared and said, "Today is born a Savior who is the Christ, the Anointed One, of God. Suddenly many angels appeared praising God and saying: "Glory to God in the highest and on earth peace to those favored by God."

Sometime later wise men came from an eastern country and worshiped the son of Mary and presented costly gifts.

According to the commandment of God the baby was presented at the temple so that Mary could offer sacrifices for cleansing after her birth. There an old man named Simeon took the baby Jesus in his arms and said, "Lord, my eyes have seen your salvation. Now let me die in peace. This child will be a light for revelation to other peoples, and for the glory of Abraham's descendants."

When Mary and Joseph had done everything required by the Law of the Lord, they returned to their hometown. There the child Jesus grew and became strong, being filled with wisdom, and the grace of God was upon him.

Comfort the Heart:

1. Do you remember from the prophet's words who would give birth to a son?
2. Whose Son would he really be?
3. Who caused the child's birth?
4. Did Joseph obey the words of the angel?
5. Where were Mary and Joseph when time came for Mary to give birth? Do you remember that place from another story? (Ruth's story)
6. Who did the angels say was born?

7. What did the old man Simeon have to say about the child? What do you think it means that the child would be a light of revelation? And that he would be for the glory of the descendants of Abraham?
8. Do you believe this was the child that God promised? Would this One be the promised person that God would use to bless all peoples?
9. The name Jesus means "God is salvation" or "Savior".
10. As the child grew whose blessing was upon him?
11. When Jesus was about age 30 he began to teach about the kingdom of God and to perform many miraculous signs and wonders. He said that he was doing the work of his Father—the work he saw God doing (John 5:19-21).

Remember the Blessing:

"...You are to give him the name Jesus, because he will save his people from their sins" (Matthew 1:21b).

An angel of the Lord appeared to them...the angel said to them, "Today in the town of David a Savior has been born to you; he is Christ the Lord" (Luke 2:9, 11).

HOPE Stories

19. Saved In a Storm

Scripture Base: Mark 4:35-41

Stir Their Thinking:

1. Imagine you are in a small boat with some friends, out on the water at night when it is very dark. Suddenly a storm blows up and there are waves that begin to fill the boat with water. The wind is strong and you cannot control the boat. There is danger the boat will sink. Will you be afraid? Who can help you at such a time? Here is a story that tells what happened to Jesus and his disciples.

Tell the Story:

Saved In a Storm

Jesus, the One who came from God, had called twelve men to follow him and be his disciples. The twelve men went with Jesus everywhere. Jesus wanted to teach them and show his disciples many things. One day Jesus had been teaching the people using stories about a farmer and his seed and other stories to teach about the kingdom of God.

When evening came Jesus said to his disciples, "Let us go to the other side of the lake." So they left the large crowd of people behind and Jesus with the disciples got into a boat.

During the night while they were crossing the lake a furious storm came up. The wind was strong and the waves began to break over the boat so that it was filling with water. Soon the boat would sink in the darkness and fierce storm.

Jesus was tired from his teaching and was asleep in the back of the boat, resting on a cushion. In their fear the disciples

85

woke Jesus and said to him, "Teacher! Teacher! Don't you care if we drown?"

Jesus stood up, rebuked the wind, and said to the waves, "Quiet! Be still!" The wind died away and the water was calm. Then Jesus said to his disciples, "Why were you so afraid? Do you still have no faith?"

The disciples were terrified and said to each other, "Who is this? Even the wind and waves obey him." That is the story from God's Word.

Comfort the Heart:

1. Why do you think that Jesus was tired and needed some quiet and rest?
2. Remember that Jesus wanted his disciples to be with him so that he could show them many things. What lesson did Jesus teach his disciples when the storm came up?
3. Do you think that Jesus was concerned and cared for his disciples so that they would not drown in the storm?
4. What did Jesus say to the wind and waves?
5. What authority do you think that Jesus had so that the wind and waves obeyed him?
6. Think for a moment like you were one of the disciples in that boat. Would you be afraid? Would you believe that Jesus could save you?
7. Could you have faith in Jesus? Many things happen to us that are like storms in our lives—sometimes bad things, sometimes things that cause great fear. Do you believe that Jesus can give you peace even when these things happen?
8. There was a follower of Jesus named Paul who wrote a letter to some friends and gave them this blessing: "Now may the Lord of peace himself give you peace at all times and in every way" (2 Thessalonians 3:16).

Remember the Blessing:

"Peace I leave with you; my peace I give you...Do not let your hearts be troubled and do not be afraid" (John 14:27).

HOPE Stories

20. Freed From an Evil Spirit

Scripture Base: Mark 5:1-20

Stir Their Thinking:

1. Demon possession is a fearful thing. The demon harms the person who is possessed, and may harm others, for the work of demons is evil.
2. Unless someone more powerful commands the demon to leave, the person is helpless.
3. There is a person the evil spirits fear for they know who he is. Here is the story from God's Word.

Tell the Story:

Freed From an Evil Spirit

One day Jesus and his disciples again crossed the lake in a boat. When Jesus stepped out of the boat, a man with an evil spirit came running to meet Jesus. This man wore no clothes and lived among the graves. No one could bind him any more, not even with a strong chain. Night and day among the graves and in the hills the man would cry out and cut himself with stones.

When he saw Jesus from a distance, the man ran and fell on his knees before Jesus. The man shouted with a loud voice, "What do you want with me, Jesus, Son of the Most High God? Swear to God that you won't torture me!"

Jesus was saying to the evil spirit, "Come out of this man, you evil spirit!" Then Jesus asked the evil spirit, "What is your name?"

The evil spirit replied, "My name is Legion, for we are many." The evil spirit begged Jesus not to send them away.

A large herd of pigs was feeding on the nearby hillside. The evil spirits begged Jesus, "Send us among the pigs; allow us to go into the pigs." So Jesus gave the evil spirits permission, and the evil spirits came out of the man and went into the pigs. The herd of pigs which was very large rushed down the steep hillside into the lake and all drowned.

Those tending the pigs ran off and reported to the people in the towns what happened. When the people came to Jesus they saw the man who had been possessed by the many evil spirits or demons, sitting there clothed and in his right mind, so they were afraid. Those who saw what happened told about the demon-possessed man—and told about the pigs as well. Then the people began to plead with Jesus to leave.

As Jesus was getting into the boat, the man who had been demon-possessed begged to go with Jesus. But Jesus did not let him. Jesus said to the man, "Go home to your family and tell them how much God has done for you, how He has had mercy on you."

So the man went away and began to tell people in all the cities how much Jesus had done for him. And all the people who heard the story were amazed. That is the end of the story from God's Word.

Comfort the Heart:

1. Who came running to meet Jesus?
2. Did the evil spirits in the man know who Jesus was? What did they say about Jesus?
3. What did the evil spirits ask Jesus not to do? Instead what did the evil spirits ask Jesus' permission to do?
4. When the people heard about what happened to the pigs and saw the man who had been demon-possessed, were they happy that the man was now healed?
5. What did the people ask Jesus to do? What did the man ask Jesus to let him do?
6. What does this story tell us about the authority of Jesus?

Remember the Blessing:

"Then Jesus came to them and said: 'All authority in heaven and on earth has been given to me'" (Matthew 28:18).

HOPE Stories

21. Hope for a Paralyzed Man

Scripture Base: John 5:1-15

Stir Their Thinking:

1. Are you helpless? Do you know someone who is not able to help themselves because of disease or some infirmity?
2. What if there were a chance to be healed but you could not act quickly enough to receive healing? Who could help you? Here is a story of how Jesus helped a man to be healed.

Tell the Story:

Hope for a Paralyzed Man

It was during feast time that Jesus went to a certain city. Now in that city near one of the city gates there is a pool of water which is surrounded by five covered porches. Here a great number of disabled people would gather and lie there—those who were blind, lame and paralyzed. It was a popular belief that from time to time an angel from God would come and stir the water. Whoever was able to get into the water first would be healed.

A man was there who had been an invalid for thirty-eight long years. Jesus saw him lying there and learned that the man had been in this condition for a long time. So Jesus asked the man, "Do you want to get well?"

The invalid man replied, "Sir, I have no one to help me into the pool when the water is stirred. While I am trying to get in, someone else goes down ahead of me."

Then Jesus said to the man, "Get up! Pick up your bed and walk." At once the man was cured; he picked up his bed and walked.

When some of the leaders heard about what happened they asked the man, "Who is this fellow who told you to pick up your bed and walk?"

The man who had been healed replied, "It was the man who made me well who told me to pick up my bed and walk." The man who was healed had no idea who had healed him, because Jesus had slipped away into the crowd of people there.

Later Jesus found the man at the place of worship and said to him, "See, you are well. Stop sinning or something worse may happen to you." The man who had been healed went away and told the leaders that it was Jesus who had made him well. That is the story from God's Word.

Comfort the Heart:

1. What were the people waiting to happen so they could be healed?
2. What did Jesus ask the invalid man?
3. When the man explained his problem, what did Jesus tell him to do?
4. What happened when the man obeyed Jesus?
5. Did the man who was healed know who Jesus was?
6. What warning did Jesus give the man?
7. What did the man who was healed tell the leaders about who healed him?
8. God says that sin is our greatest sickness. Do you want to get well?
9. Would you do what Jesus tells you to do?
10. Would you tell others what Jesus did for you?

Remember the Blessing:

"He forgives all my sins and heals all my diseases" (Psalm 103:3).

HOPE Stories

22. Helped By a Good Neighbor

Scripture Base: Luke 10:25-37; 2 Kings 17:24-41

Stir Their Thinking:

1. Has some misfortune happened to you? Who helped you?
2. Would you be surprised if someone you thought was not a worthy person helped you?
3. Long ago in the land where Jesus lived there were people called Samaritans who lived mostly in a certain part of the country. They were disliked by other people who thought them to be unworthy persons. For long before many of the Samaritans had intermarried with foreigners and took the religion of the foreigners. So others looked down at the Samaritans as low caste people.

Tell the Story:

Helped By a Good Neighbor

A man who was an expert in the law came to test Jesus. He said, "Teacher, what must I do to inherit eternal life?"

Jesus asked the man, "What is written in the law?"

The man replied, "Love the Lord your God with all your heart and with all your soul and with all your strength and with all your mind. And, love your neighbor as you love yourself."

"You have answered well," Jesus said. "Do this and you will live."

But the man wanted to justify himself, so he asked Jesus, "And who is my neighbor?"

So Jesus told this story: "A certain man was going down from this city to another city down the mountain. Along the way the man happened to fall into the hands of robbers. The

91

robbers beat him and took his clothes, leaving the man half dead. Then the robbers went away.

There was a priest who happened to be going down the same road. When he saw the wounded man, the priest passed by on the other side and continued on his way. So another man came along who also helped in worship. When he saw the wounded man he also passed by on the other side without stopping.

But a Samaritan, as he traveled, came to where the wounded man lay and saw him and took pity on him. The Samaritan went to the wounded man and bandaged his wounds, pouring in medicine. Then he put the man on his own donkey and took the wounded man to an inn and took care of him. The next day the Samaritan took out some money and gave it to the innkeeper and said, "Look after this wounded man. When I return I will pay you for any extra expense you may have."

Then Jesus asked the expert in the law, "Which of these three do you think was a good neighbor to the man who fell into the hands of robbers?"

The expert in the law replied, "The one who had mercy on the wounded man."

Jesus told the expert in the law, "Go and do likewise."

Comfort the Heart:

1. Are there some people you think are unworthy?
2. Would you accept help from them if some misfortune happened to you?
3. Who do you consider to be a good neighbor?
4. Are you a good neighbor to those who need help?
5. Who gave the most hope and help to the wounded man?
6. What if a man, who was not of your own people, helped you by suffering and even dying for your wrongdoing, would you accept help from him? Soon you will hear what Jesus as a good neighbor did for you.

Remember the Blessing:

"For the Son of Man came to seek and to save what was lost." (Luke 19:10)

23. Hope and Forgiveness for a Sinner

Scripture Base: Luke 7:36-50

Stir Their Thinking:

1. If someone forgave your debts or offences against them, how would you express your gratitude?
2. Have you ever judged another person who you thought was not a worthy person? What if they did something that showed they were truly thankful in their hearts?

Tell the Story:

Hope and Forgiveness for a Sinner

One of the righteous people named Simon had invited Jesus to his home for a meal. Some of the man's friends were there, too, eating around the table. A woman who had lived a sinful life in that town learned that Jesus was eating at Simon's house. She came bringing a jar of expensive perfume and stood at the feet of Jesus weeping and began to wet Jesus' feet with her tears. Then the woman wiped the feet of Jesus with her hair, kissed Jesus' feet, and poured perfume on his feet.

When the man who had invited Jesus saw what was happening, he said to himself, "If this Jesus were really a prophet, he would know who is touching him and what kind of woman she is—that she is a sinner!"

Jesus knew what the man was thinking, so Jesus said to the man, "Simon, I have something to tell you."

"Tell me, Teacher," Simon replied.

Then Jesus told this story: "Two men owed money to a certain moneylender. One man owed a very large sum of money. The other man owed only a small amount of money. Neither of the two men had the money to repay their debts. So the moneylender cancelled the debts of both men." Then Jesus asked Simon, "Now which of these two men will love the moneylender more?"

Simon replied, "I suppose the one who had the bigger debt canceled."

"You have answered correctly," Jesus said. Then Jesus turned toward the woman and said to Simon, "Do you see this woman? I came into your house and you did not give me any water to wash my feet. But this woman wet my feet with her tears and wiped them with her hair. Simon, you did not give me a friendly kiss of greeting. But this woman, from the time I entered, has not stopped kissing my feet. Simon, you did not put any fragrant oil on my head, but this woman has poured perfume on my feet. Therefore, I tell you, her many sins have been forgiven for she loved much. But he who has been forgiven little loves little."

Then Jesus said to the woman, "Your sins are forgiven."

The other guests began to say among themselves, "Who is this who even forgives sins?"

Jesus said to the woman, "Your faith has saved you. Go in peace." That is the end of the story from God's Word.

Comfort the Heart:

1. Was Simon considered a good man among his people?
2. Was the woman considered a good person among the people?
3. How did she show that she was sorry for the wrong things she had done?
4. Did Simon think this was a good thing to do?
5. In the story Jesus told, who loved the moneylender more?
6. Who had done more for Jesus, Simon or the woman?
7. Who do you think loved Jesus more?
8. What did Jesus do for the woman?
9. What do you think Jesus could do for you?

Remember the Blessing:

"If we confess our sins, he is faithful and just and will forgive us our sins and purify us from all unrighteousness" (1 John 1:9).

HOPE Stories

24. Hope for an Unclean Woman

Scripture Base: Mark 5:21-34; Leviticus 15:25-28

Stir Their Thinking:

1. Do you know anyone who is considered unclean?
2. What happens if an unclean person touches something or someone? What must be done?
3. What hope is there for an unclean person?
4. *Note for the storyer:* In Jesus' time and even today in many third world countries a woman with a bloody discharge is like a living dead woman. She is unclean, and being unclean, she cannot enter a place of worship, cook food for a man to eat, any place when she sits or lies is unclean and must be purified, and in many cases, anyone she touches is polluted—especially a holy person. She could be stoned for polluting such a person. (See Leviticus 15:19-30.)

Tell the Story:

Hope for an Unclean Woman

A large crowd was gathered around Jesus who was with his disciples. As they walked along the crowd of people pressed around Jesus. In the crowd was a woman who had been subject to bleeding for twelve years. She had suffered a great deal under the care of many doctors and had spent all the money she had. Instead of getting better, the woman grew worse. When she heard about Jesus, the woman came up behind Jesus in the crowd and touched Jesus' cloak. She was thinking, "If I can just touch Jesus' clothes, I will be healed." Immediately her bleeding stopped and the woman felt in her body that she was freed from her suffering.

At once Jesus realized that power had gone out from him. Jesus turned around in the crowd and asked, "Who touched my clothes?"

Jesus' disciples answered, "You see the people crowding around you. And yet how can you ask, 'Who touched me?'"

But Jesus kept looking around to see who had touched him. Then the woman, knowing what had happened to her, came and fell at the feet of Jesus and, trembling with fear, told Jesus the whole truth.

Then Jesus said to the woman, "Daughter, your faith has healed you. Go in peace and be freed from your suffering." That is the story from God's Word.

Comfort the Heart:

1. Was the woman's disease getting any better? How long had she had the disease? Would you consider her to be without any hope?
2. Why do you think the woman wanted to touch Jesus? Do you think she believed that Jesus was powerful to heal her—even if she just touched his clothes?
3. What happened when the woman did touch Jesus' clothes?
4. Did Jesus know that someone had touched him? What did Jesus feel when the woman touched him?
5. Why do you think Jesus wanted to know who touched him? Why do you think the woman tried to hide in the crowd? (She had ritually polluted not only Jesus but all she had touched in the crowd. There would be anger.)
6. What did Jesus say had healed the woman? What blessing did Jesus give the woman?
7. What do you think Jesus can do for you if you could just touch him? Jesus is not with us on earth today. He is in heaven. But we can still touch him in faith by believing in him.
8. Do you know that sin makes us unclean? If we touch Jesus in faith by believing in him we can be made clean. Then we can go in peace, too.

Remember the Blessing:

"...The blood of Jesus, his (God's) Son, purifies us from all sin" (1 John 1:7).

25. Sight for a Blind Man

Scripture Base: Mark 10:46-52; John 9

Stir Their Thinking:

1. Is anyone in the group blind? Have them tell what it is like to be blind.
2. What kinds of work can a blind person do? Or must they resort to begging to live?
3. What if someone offered them a chance to see? What changes might be in their lives?

Tell the Story:

Sight for a Blind Man

As Jesus and his disciples were leaving a certain city, a large crowd was following. Along the way sat a blind man named Bartimaeus who was begging. When Bartimaeus heard that it was Jesus who was passing by, he began to shout, "Jesus, have mercy on me!" Many of the people in the crowd rebuked Bartimaeus, telling him to be quiet. But Bartimaeus shouted even louder, "Have mercy on me!"

Jesus heard Bartimaeus' shouts and stopped and said, "Call him."

So the people called to the blind man saying, "Cheer up! On your feet! He is calling you." Bartimaeus threw his cloak aside, jumped to his feet, and came to Jesus.

Jesus asked the blind man, "What do you want me to do for you?"

Bartimaeus said, "Lord, I want to see."

"Go," Jesus said, "your faith has healed you." Immediately Bartimaeus received his sight and followed Jesus along the road while praising God. When the people saw what happened, they also praised God.

At another time as Jesus walked along he saw a blind man who was blind from birth. Jesus' disciples asked, "Teacher, who sinned, this man or his parents, that he was born blind?"

Jesus replied, "This is not because either the man sinned or his parents. But it happened so that the work of God might be displayed in the man's life." Then Jesus spat on the ground and made some mud with his saliva, and put it on the man's eyes. Then Jesus said to the man, "Now go wash in the pool." The man went to the pool, washed his eyes, and came home seeing.

The man's neighbors and those who had seen him begging asked, "Is this the same man who used to sit and beg?" Some said that it was. Others said, "No, he only looks like him."

But the man insisted, "I am the same man."

"Then how are your eyes now opened?" they asked.

The man who could now see said, "The man they call Jesus made some mud and put it on my eyes. He told me to go to the pool and wash. So I went and washed and then I could see."

Some of the religious leaders did not believe the man had been born blind and now received his sight. They sent for the man's parents and asked, "Is this your son?" The man's parents answered, "We know he is our son. And we know he was born blind. But how he can now see or who opened his eyes we don't know. Our son is of age, ask him. He will speak for himself."

Later when Jesus found the man he asked him, "Do you believe in the Son of Man?"

"Who is he, sir? Tell me so that I may believe in him," the man said.

Jesus said to the man, "You have now seen him. In fact, he is the one speaking to you."

Then the man said, "Lord, I believe." And the man who had been born blind but now could see worshiped Jesus.

That is the end of the stories from God's Word

Comfort the Heart:

1. In the first story what did Bartimaeus do when he heard that it was Jesus who was passing by?
2. Did Jesus hear Bartimaeus?
3. What did Bartimaeus want from Jesus?
4. When Bartimaeus received his sight what did Jesus say to him? What do you think Jesus meant by saying, "Your faith has healed you"?
5. What did Bartimaeus do as he followed Jesus along the road?
6. In the second story the man was born blind, what did the disciples think caused the man's blindness?
7. What did Jesus say about the man's blindness?
8. What unusual thing did Jesus do to the man?
9. What command did Jesus give the man?
10. Did the man obey Jesus? What happened when he obeyed Jesus?
11. Did the man know who Jesus was? Do you know who Jesus is?
12. Did the man believe in Jesus after he learned it was Jesus talking to him?
13. What would it take for you also to believe in Jesus?

Remember the Blessing:

Then Jesus told the disciple named Thomas: "Because you have seen me, you have believed; blessed are those who have not seen and yet have believed" (John 20:20).

26. Living Water for
A Thirsty Woman and Her People

Scripture Base: John 4:4-30, 39-42

Stir Their Thinking:

1. Refer to the summary about the Samaritans from the *Helped By A Good Neighbor* story. Many in countries where Hindus live (and other Asians) have a very clear understanding about the caste system.
2. Have you ever heard about "living water" that satisfies your soul? In this story Jesus offers living water to a thirsty woman and her people.

Tell the Story:

Living Water for a Thirsty Woman
And Her People

Jesus and his disciples chose to pass through the land where the Samaritan people lived. As he came to a certain town there was a well there dug in the days of Abraham's grandson. Jesus was tired from his journey and sat down by the well to rest. When a Samaritan woman came to draw water, Jesus said to her, "Will you give me a drink?"

The Samaritan woman said to Jesus, "I am a Samaritan woman, how can you ask me for a drink? "

Jesus answered the woman, "If you knew the gift of God, and who it is that asks you for a drink, you would instead ask him and he would give you living water."

"Sir," the woman replied, "you have nothing to use in drawing water. The well is deep. Where can you get this living water? Are you greater than our ancestor who gave us this well and drank from it himself, as did also his sons and his flocks and herds?"

Jesus answered, "Everyone who drinks this water will thirst again. But whoever drinks the water I give him will never thirst. Indeed, the water will become in him a spring of water bubbling up to eternal life."

Now the woman said to Jesus, "Sir, give me some of this water so that I won't get thirsty and have to return here to draw more water."

Jesus told her, "Go, call your husband and come back."

"I have no husband," the woman replied.

Jesus said to her, "You have answered truthfully when you say that you have no husband. The fact is, you've had five husbands and the man you live with now is not your husband. What you have said is quite true."

The woman defended herself saying, "I can see that you are a prophet. Our ancestors worshiped here on this mountain but your people say we must worship in your temple."

Jesus declared, "A time is coming when you will worship God neither here or in our temple. True worshipers will worship God the Father in spirit and truth. For they are the kind of worshipers the Father seeks. God is spirit, his worshipers must worship in spirit and truth."

The woman said, "I know that God's Anointed One (called Christ) is coming. When he comes he will explain everything to us."

Then Jesus declared, "I who speak to you am the Anointed One."

The woman left her water jar and went back to the town and said to the people, "Come see a man who told me everything I ever did. Could he be God's Anointed One?" The people came out of the town to see Jesus. Many of the Samaritans in that town believed in Jesus because of the woman's testimony. Jesus stayed with them two more days, and because of his words many more believed in him.

The people said to the woman, "We no longer believe just because of what you said. Now we have heard for ourselves, and we know this man really is the Savior of the world." That is the end of the story from God's Word.

Comfort the Heart:

1. What did Jesus ask the woman to give him?
2. Do you think Jesus knew about the woman and was testing her?
3. Where did the woman think Jesus would get his water?
4. Where would the living water that Jesus spoke about come from?
5. Was the woman expecting God's Anointed One (the Christ) to come? What did she say he would do when he came?
6. Who did Jesus say was God's Anointed One (the Christ)?
7. What did the woman's testimony cause some of her people to do?
8. What did Jesus' words cause others to do?
9. Are you thirsty? Would you like a drink of this living water? Jesus said, "Come to me and drink." He was talking about believing in Jesus as God's Anointed Son who was come into the world to forgive sin and provide eternal life for you and me, just as he did for the Samaritan woman and her people.

Remember the Blessing:

"If a man is thirsty, let him come to me and drink. Whoever believes in me, as the Scripture has said, streams of living water will flow from within him" (John 7:37b-38).

"...whoever drinks the water I give him will never thirst."
(John 4:14a).

HOPE Stories
27. Compassion for the Hungry

Scripture Base: Mark 6:30-44

Stir Their Thinking:

1. When you are hungry, where can you find food?
2. Who could feed a very large number of people in a remote place? Here is a story about a time when Jesus fed a very large number of people who had come to hear his teaching.

Tell the Story:

Compassion for the Hungry

Jesus and his disciples went away by themselves in a boat to a solitary place to get some rest. But many people saw Jesus leaving and recognized him and ran on foot ahead of Jesus. When Jesus and his disciples landed and saw the large crowd, Jesus had compassion on them, because they were like sheep without a shepherd. So Jesus began teaching the people many things.

By this time it was late in the day. So the disciples came to Jesus and said, "This is a remote place and it's already very late. Send the people away so they can go to some place and buy something to eat."

But Jesus answered the disciples, "You give them something to eat."

The disciples protested, "It would take eight month's of a man's wages! Are we to go and spend that much money to buy food and give it to the people to eat?"

Jesus asked, "How many loaves of bread do you have? Go and see."

When the disciples had found out, they said, "We found five loaves of bread and two fish."

Jesus directed the disciples to have the people sit down in groups on the green grass. Then Jesus took the five loaves of bread and two fish, and looked up to heaven and gave thanks. Jesus broke the loaves and gave them to the disciples to set before the people. Jesus also divided the two fish among all the people. Everyone ate and were satisfied. Afterward, the disciples picked up the remaining scraps of bread and fish that filled twelve baskets. The number of men who had eaten that day was very great. That is the story from God's Word.

Comfort the Heart:

1. Why do you think the people followed Jesus?
2. When Jesus saw the people, did he send them away? What did Jesus do instead?
3. When it was late in the day the disciples were concerned about the people. What did the disciples want Jesus to do?
4. Instead what did Jesus tell the disciples to do?
5. Before Jesus gave the bread and fish to the people to eat, what did he do?
6. Was there enough food for everyone to eat? How much food remained after everyone finished eating?
7. That day Jesus was feeding the peoples' hungry hearts with his teaching. But he was also concerned with their hungry bodies. As a shepherd watches over his sheep and sees that they have plenty to eat, so Jesus watches over those who believe in him, to provide their needs.

Remember the Blessing:

"For the bread of God is he who comes down from heaven and gives life to the world...I am the bread of life. He who comes to me will never go hungry, and he who believes in me will never be thirsty" (John 6:33, 35).

HOPE Stories

28. Life for the Dead

Scripture Base: John 11:1-45

Stir Their Thinking:

1. Talk about the death of loved ones. Talk about our inability to keep them from dying or to raise them to life again.
2. Who can comfort us when a family member or friend dies?
3. Who alone has authority over life and death?

Tell the Story:

Life for the Dead

Lazarus and his two sisters Mary and Martha were friends of Jesus. Lazarus became sick so the sisters sent word to Jesus saying, "Lord, your friend Lazarus is sick."

When Jesus heard this, he said to his disciples, "This sickness will not end in death. No, it is for God's glory and to glorify God's Son." Jesus loved Lazarus and his family, and yet when he heard that Lazarus was sick, Jesus stayed in that place two more days. Then he said to his disciples, "Our friend Lazarus has fallen asleep, I am going there to wake him up."

Jesus' disciples said, "Lord, if Lazarus is sleeping, that means he will get well." Jesus had been speaking of Lazarus' death, but the disciples thought Jesus meant sleep.

So then Jesus told the disciples plainly, "Lazarus is dead. Let us go to him."

When Jesus arrived at the village he found that Lazarus had already been dead four days. Many friends had come from the nearby city to comfort Mary and Martha. When Martha heard that Jesus was coming she went out to meet him, but Mary stayed at home. Martha said to Jesus, "Lord, if only you had been here, my brother would not have died. But I know that God will give you whatever you ask."

Jesus said to Martha, "Your brother will rise again."

Martha answered, "I know he will rise again in the resurrection at the last day."

Jesus said to Martha, "I am the resurrection and the life. He who believes in me will live, even though he dies. And whoever lives and believes in me will never die. Do you believe this?"

"Yes, Lord," Martha told Jesus, "I believe that you are the Christ, God's Anointed One, the Son of God, who was to come into the world." Then Martha went back to tell Mary, "The Teacher is here, and he is asking for you."

When Mary heard that Jesus was there, she quickly went out to meet him and said, "Lord, if only you had been here, my brother would not have died."

When Jesus saw Mary weeping and her friends weeping also, he was deeply moved and troubled in his spirit. Then Jesus asked, "Where have you laid his body?"

At the grave Jesus said, "Remove the covering."

Martha protested, "But, Lord, there will be a bad smell for Lazarus has been there four days."

"Didn't I tell you that if you believed, you would see the glory of God?" Jesus said. So the stone covering to the grave was removed.

Then Jesus looked up toward heaven and prayed, "Father, I thank you because you always hear me. I am praying now so that the people will believe that you sent me." Then Jesus called in a loud voice, "Lazarus, come out!"

The dead man came out still wrapped in the grave cloths. Many of the friends who came to visit Mary, when they saw what Jesus did, put their faith in Jesus. But others who doubted and did not believe went to report to the jealous religious leaders what Jesus had done. That ends the story from God's Word.

Comfort the Heart:

1. Did Jesus know that Lazarus was going to die?
2. Did Jesus believe that he could bring Lazarus back to life again?
3. What did Martha say to Jesus when he arrived at her village? Did she have faith in Jesus?
4. What did Jesus say about the life and the resurrection? Do you know what this means? It means that Jesus is Lord of both the living and the dead—over both life and death.
5. The people at that time believed that when a person died their spirit remained near the body for three days or until there was a bad odor. By the fourth day the person was really dead. Was Lazarus really dead?
6. What did Jesus say would happen if Martha really believed?
7. What did Jesus say when he prayed before calling to Lazarus? Did the Father in heaven always hear Jesus?
8. What did Jesus say to Lazarus? Did Lazarus hear Jesus' voice?
9. When the friends of Mary and Martha saw what Jesus did, what did some of them do? What did those who doubted do?
10. What do you believe about Jesus? Could you believe like Martha and say what she said: "I know that you are God's Anointed One, the Son of God, who was to come into the world"?

Remember the Blessing:

Jesus said, "I am the resurrection and the life. He who believes in me will live, even though he dies; and whoever lives and believes in me will never die" (John 11:25).

HOPE Stories

29. Words of Comfort and Hope

Scripture Base: Mark 10:33-34; Luke 22:15-20; John 13:33-14:21

Stir Their Thinking:

1. What do you say to people when you are going away?
2. Jesus had been with his disciples for over three years, teaching them many things. Now Jesus tells his disciples that he must go away. This story is what Jesus told his disciples to comfort them and give them hope.

Tell the Story:

Words of Comfort and Hope

Many times Jesus told his disciples that he would be betrayed and arrested, falsely accused, beaten and mocked and put to death. But he would live again on the third day. Now the time had come for this to happen. It was also the time for a special feast that reminded the people of the time when God rescued them from slavery in the land of Egypt.

Jesus had gathered with his disciples to eat a last meal together and to celebrate the feast. After eating Jesus took some bread and asked God to bless it. Then Jesus broke the bread and gave it to his disciples to eat and said, "This is my body given for you. Eat this to remember me." In the same way, Jesus took the cup of drink and said, "This cup is the new covenant in my blood, which is poured out for you, and for the sins of many." Drink from it, all of you.

Then Jesus began to teach his disciples saying, "My children, I will be with you only a little longer. Where I am going you cannot follow now, but you will follow later."

111

The disciple named Peter asked, "Why can't I follow you now? I will even lay down my life for you."

Jesus continued his teaching, "Do not let your hearts be troubled. Trust in God; trust also in me. In my Father's house are many rooms; I am going there to prepare a place for you. And I will come back and take you to be with me so you may be where I am. You know the way to the place I am going.

The disciple named Thomas said to Jesus, "Lord, we don't know where you are going. How can we know the way?"

Jesus answered, "I am the way and the truth and the life. No one comes to the Father except through me."

Another disciple named Phillip said, "Lord, show us the Father and that will be enough for us."

Jesus answered: "Don't you know me, Phillip, even after I have been with you such a long time? Anyone who has seen me has seen the Father. The words I say to you are not just my own. It is the Father living in me doing his work."

Then Jesus said that if he went away he would send in his place a Comforter, the Spirit of truth from the Father. And Jesus said, "If anyone loves me, he will obey my teaching. My Father will love him too. He who does not obey me does not love me. I give you my peace. So let not your hearts be troubled and do not be afraid." The end of the story.

Comfort the Heart:

1. Sharing a meal is a good time to talk. What did Jesus say was the meaning of the cup of drink?
2. Why did Jesus say that he was going away? What would he do for his disciples?
3. What do you think Jesus meant when he said that he was the way, the truth and the life?
4. Jesus went away to prepare a place for you and for me in his Father's house. But we must believe in Jesus as God's Son and as our Savior who died for our sins.

Remember the Blessing:

"I am the way the truth and the life. No one comes to the Father except through me" (John 14:6).

30. Father, Forgive Them

Scripture Base: Luke 22

Stir Their Thinking:

1. Has anyone ever betrayed you? Have you betrayed anyone or know someone who was betrayed?
2. What if someone did really bad things to you or your family? Could you forgive them?
3. In this story we will see that Jesus was betrayed by a friend, beaten, mocked and put to death. But Jesus forgave those who did this to him. Could you?

Tell the Story:

Father Forgive Them

It was beginning to happen just as Jesus had said. One of the disciples named Judas went to betray Jesus to the jealous religious leaders. At night when Jesus had gone to a quiet garden to pray, the leaders and guards came to arrest Jesus. He was brought before the ruling religious leaders to be questioned. Many false witnesses came to give testimony against Jesus. But their testimonies were not in agreement. Then the high priest asked Jesus, "Tell us plainly, are you the Son of the Most High God?"

Jesus replied, "I am." So it was agreed that Jesus was worthy of death because they believed that Jesus was speaking blasphemy against God by claiming to be God.

Later Jesus was brought before the foreign governor who also questioned Jesus but could find no reason to put him to death. When the governor tried to release Jesus the religious leaders shouted, "Crucify him! Let his blood be upon us and our children." So the governor gave Jesus over to his soldiers to beat him and mock him and then to put Jesus to death.

115

That same day Jesus was crucified, being nailed to a wooden cross between two criminals to die along with them. The religious leaders were standing there saying, "He saved others; let him save himself if he is truly the Christ of God, the Chosen One."

Jesus prayed for those who were crucifying him and mocking him saying, "Father, forgive them. They don't know what they are doing."

One of the criminals mocked Jesus saying, "Aren't you the Christ? Save yourself and save us!"

The other criminal rebuked the first one saying, "Don't you fear God? We are punished justly for our deeds. But this man has done nothing wrong." Then he said, "Jesus, remember me when you come into your kingdom."

Jesus replied, "Today you will be with me in paradise."

Soon it became very dark as the sun stopped shining. Jesus cried out in a loud voice, "My God, why have you forsaken me?" For Jesus was taking upon himself the guilt and sins of all people. At last the sacrifice was completed and Jesus cried out, "It is finished! Father, into your hands I give my spirit." At that Jesus bowed his head and died. One of the soldiers had pierced the side of Jesus to see if he were really dead. The soldier in charge, when he heard Jesus' cry and saw what happened said, "Surely this man was the Son of God!"

Two secret followers of Jesus claimed his body and prepared it for burial in a nearby unused rich man's tomb. The opening was sealed with a large stone. It had all happened just as the prophet had said would happen. This is the story from God's Word.

Comfort the Heart:

1. Jesus knew he was going to die. What did he tell his disciples would happen to him soon?

2. When the high priest asked Jesus if he were the Son of the Most High God, what did Jesus say?
3. Did the foreign governor find Jesus guilty of any crime?
4. When the governor wanted to release Jesus what did the leaders demand?
5. How was Jesus to be put to death?
6. What did the two criminals who were also being put to death have to say to Jesus?
7. Do you know why Jesus cried out, "My God, why have you forsaken me?" Jesus was speaking the words from the holy writings (see Psalm 22:1). At this time Jesus was taking upon himself the sin of all people. God in heaven who is holy and righteous without sin could no longer look upon his Son who was now bearing our sin (see Habakkuk 1:13). Jesus was the Lamb of God, the sacrificial animal that was being sacrificed for our sin (see John 1:29). After God accepted the sacrifice Jesus again cried out, "It is finished!" Then he again called God "Father" (see Psalm 1:7) and asked God to receive his spirit as Jesus died.
8. Jesus was nailed to a wooden cross with nails through his hands and feet. After Jesus died a soldier pierced Jesus' side. The prophets had said that God's Anointed One would be pierced (see Psalm 22:16; Zechariah 12:10).
9. What did the soldier in charge of the crucifixion say after he heard the words of Jesus and saw all that happened?
10. If you had been there what would you have said?
11. Now that you have heard this story and the others about Jesus, what do you believe about Jesus?
12. We are going to talk about what Jesus wants you to do now that you have heard his story.

Remember the Blessing:

"God so loved the world that he gave his one and only Son, that whoever believes in him shall not perish but have eternal life" (John 3:16).

31. What Must We Do To Be Saved?

Scripture Base: Luke 14:16-24;15:1-2, 11-24

Stir Their Thinking:

1. Have you ever offended your father in some way? If you did, and found yourself in great need, could you return to him and ask his forgiveness? Would he forgive you?
2. If you were invited to a great feast and when it was ready you said that you would not attend, would that be a good thing to do? What might happen?

Tell the Story:

What Must We Do To Be Saved?

Once when some religious leaders saw people they considered to be sinners gathering around Jesus, the leaders said, "This man welcomes sinners and eats with them." Jesus heard what the leaders were saying. So Jesus told this story:

There was a man who had two sons. one day the younger son said to his father, "Father, give me my share of the inheritance." So the father divided his property between his older and younger sons.

Not long after that, the younger son got together all that he had and set off for a distant country. There the younger son wasted all his wealth in foolish living. After he had used up all his money, there was a severe famine in that whole country, and the son became very hungry and needy. So he went to a certain man who hired the son to feed his pigs. The son longed to fill his stomach with the same food the pigs were eating. For no one gave him anything to eat.

When the son came to his senses, he said, "How many of my father's servants have food to spare? Here I am starving to death! I will set out and go back to my father and say to him: 'Father, I have sinned against heaven and against you. I am no longer worthy to be called your son; make me one of your hired servants.'" So the son got up and went to his father.

But while the younger son was still a long way off, his father saw him coming and was filled with compassion for his son. So the father ran to meet his son, threw his arms around his son and kissed him.

The son said, "Father, I have sinned against heaven and against you. I am no longer worthy to be called your son."

But the father said to his servants, "Quick! Bring the best robe and put it on him. Put a ring on his finger and shoes on his feet. Prepare food for a feast. Let us celebrate! This son of mine was dead and is now alive again; he was lost and is now found." So the father and servants began to celebrate.

Earlier Jesus told another story and at the end said, "I tell you there is rejoicing in heaven over one sinner who repents." Then at another time Jesus told the story of a great feast and what happened when the people were invited to come and eat.

A certain man was preparing a great feast and invited many guests. At the time of the banquet he sent his servants to tell those who had been invited, "Come, for now the meal is ready."

But all those invited began to make excuses. The first said, "I have just bought a field and must now go and see it. Please excuse me if I do not come." Another said, "I have just bought some oxen and I'm on my way to try them out. Please excuse me." Still another said, "I have just married, so I can't come."

The servant came back and reported this to his master. Then the owner of the house became angry and ordered his servant: "Go quickly into the streets and alleys of the town and bring in the poor, the crippled, and the blind." When the servant reported that he had invited those but there was still room. The master said, "Go out and bring others in so that my house may be full."

Jesus said to the crowds, "Come unto me, all you who are weary and burdened, and I will give you rest" (Matthew 11:28). That is the story from God's Word.

Comfort the Heart:

1. In the first story do you think the younger son offended his father by demanding his inheritance, even while his father lived?
2. Did he use his inheritance wisely? What happened when it was all gone?
3. What did the younger son decide to do? What was he going to say to his father?
4. Was the father watching and waiting for his son to return?
5. When the father saw the son coming what did his do?
6. Was the father happy to see his son again? What did he have to say about his son's return?
7. The son repented of his wrongdoing and was forgiven by his father. Is this a good thing to happen?
8. In the second story Jesus told about a wonderful feast that a man had prepared and then invited his friends. When the feast was ready what did those invited say?
9. Was the man who prepared the feast happy? What did he instruct his servants to do?
10. The lesson you can learn in these stories is that even when we have offended our Father in heaven, that is God, he eagerly awaits out repenting of sin and return to him. In the story about the death of Jesus did you see that Jesus took our punishment for wrongdoing upon himself. So we are welcome to return to God, our heavenly Father.
11. In the second story did you learn that God has prepared a great blessing for us. But many make excuses and so do not accept what God has prepared.

12. Like the younger son we must realize that we have offended God, repent of our sin and confess it, and return to God who waits to forgive. Jesus has already paid for our sin. If we do not accept what God has prepared for us, He has invited others to receive it.
13. God's greatest blessing is forgiveness of our sins and the promise of eternal life with him. We receive this by believing on Jesus, God's Son, as Savior and accepting God's forgiveness for our sin.

Remember the Blessing:

"If we claim to be without sin, we deceive ourselves and the truth is not in us. If we confess our sins, *God* is faithful and just and will forgive our sins and purify us from all unrighteousness" (1 John 1:8-9).

"...Jesus Christ, the Righteous One...He is the atoning sacrifice for our sins, and not only for ours but also for the sins of the whole world" (1 John 2:1b-2).

Note: *I have used these two stories because they speak across cultures. There may be other stories that you feel are better for drawing the net among your listeners. You should choose the stories which you think best appeal to your listeners, speaking to their worldviews, and help them to understand about confessing they are sinners who need forgiveness, that God stands ready and waiting to forgive, and that there are consequences for refusing the blessing God has prepared for all who will accept it.*

If you have another set of evangelism Scriptures now is the time to share them and invite a response.

32. No More Suffering and Sorrow

Scripture Base: Revelation 7:9-17; 20:15; 21:3-4, 27; 22:1-5, 8, 14

Stir Their Thinking:

1. What do you believe about life beyond the grave? Will it be a good life? What has God promised for those who confess their sin and believe on Jesus as their Savior?
2. If you have not yet made this decision then you need to listen to the story which is the true testimony of a vision that one of Jesus' disciples had. The story is recorded in the Bible for us today to remind us of God's blessing.
3. For those who suffer and sorrow today there is hope for the future.

Tell the Story:

No More Suffering and Sorrow

John, one of the disciples of Jesus, when he was an old man and suffering in exile for his faith in Jesus, had a wonderful vision of the future. For God revealed to John in a vision what was going to happen at the end of the age after Jesus had returned to claim his followers, just as Jesus promised his disciples.

John saw Jesus in all his glory as the resurrected Lamb of God who had shed his blood for the sins of all who would believe on him.

In the vision John saw a great multitude of people in white robes standing before Jesus, the Lamb of God. The people were from every nation, tribe, people and language. They were holding palm branches in their hands, worshiping and crying out: "Salvation belongs to our God, who sits on the throne, and to the Lamb."

Then John was told these were the people who were clothed in robes washed clean by the blood of the Lamb. Never again will they hunger; never again will they thirst. The sun will not beat upon them, nor any scorching heat. For the Lamb at the center of the throne will be their shepherd. He will lead them to springs of living water. God will wipe away every tear from their eyes.

John heard and saw many things about the coming judgment of unbelievers and the punishment awaiting them. For if anyone's name was not written in the Lamb's book of life, he was thrown into the lake of fire.

Then John saw a new heaven and a new earth. A loud voice proclaimed, "Now the dwelling of God is with men, and he will live with them. They will be his people, and he will be their God. He will wipe every tear from their eyes. There will be no more death or mourning or crying or pain, for all the old things are passed away...To him who is thirsty I will give to drink without cost from the spring of the water of life...In the new city nothing impure will ever enter it, nor will anyone who does what is shameful or deceitful. Only those whose names are written in the Lamb's book of life will enter."

Then the angel showed John the river of the water of life, clear as crystal, flowing from the throne of God and the Lamb. On each side of the river stood the tree of life, bearing its fruit every month. The leaves of the tree are for healing of the nations. No longer will there be any curse and no more night. The Lord God will be their light.

Then John said, "I am the one who heard and saw these things."

Then Jesus said, "Blessed are those who wash their robes, that they may have the right to the tree of life and may go through the gates into the city. I have sent my angel to give you this testimony." That is the story from God's Word.

Comfort the Heart:

1. This story is a warning to those who refuse God's offer of forgiveness of sins. Those whose names are written in the Lamb's book of life are forgiven their sins.
2. What are some things promised for those who are forgiven?
3. In the story what reminds us that ALL peoples are invited.
4. I will be there. Will you be there?

Remember the Blessing:

"He will wipe every tear from their eyes. There will be no more death or mourning or crying or pain, for the old order of things has passed away" (Revelation 21:4).

Note: *This is another opportunity to explain about salvation with the forgiveness of our sins. Since this story series was conceived for those who suffer and have great need, the theme of eternal relief from suffering and the future state of blessedness for believers may appeal to many.*

Many Muslims need to have this story on judgment and the true blessed state of those who believe in Jesus to counter what they believe about the judgment and Paradise.

You may need to be patient with some who live in such dire need that even tomorrow is a distant future—how much more can they even imagine a time out there when after death they will find relief. In my experience I have found that for these folks salvation must be presented as an "immediate" benefit and not as we sometimes say—Pie in the sky by and by.

For some, salvation is acceptance and relationship. So the Prodigal Son story can be powerful. For others the idea of the fellowship meal is a picture of being satisfied and having the fellowship of eating together. All of these aspects come from your listeners' worldviews.

For others forgiveness of wrongdoing does not come easily in their cultures. They need to know that in Jesus there is forgiveness.

And for many who are crippled, disfigured, handicapped or sick there is a message of hope for a better day in the company and presence of our God and Jesus our Savior.

33. Asking for God's Help

Scripture Base: Mark 1:40-45; Luke 7:1-10; Luke 18:35-43.

Stir Their Thinking:

1. In the beginning, when God created the world, it was a place of peace as all lived in harmony. There was no need for God provided the food. But when Adam and Eve disobeyed God, things changed, sin came into the human family. And a curse came upon the earth.
2. There are many stories in the Bible that tell us how God wants us to turn to him to provide our needs. God loves us and cares for us. In some of the stories we saw how God allowed certain things to happen so the people would turn to him for help.
3. Here are stories of those in great need who came to God's Son Jesus for help.

Tell the Story:

Asking for God's Help

In the days of Jesus leprosy was a terrible disease. It was required for lepers to cover their face and to avoid people while crying, "Unclean! Unclean!" One day as Jesus traveled through his home province a man with leprosy came to Jesus and begged on his knees saying, "If you are willing, you can make me clean."

Jesus was filled with compassion for the man and reached out his hand and touched the man with leprosy. Jesus said, "I am willing. Be clean!" Immediately the leprosy left the man and he was cured. Jesus sent the man away at once with a strong warning, "See to it that you tell no one what has happened to you. But go, show yourself to the priest and offer the proper sacrifice for cleansing as required." Instead the man went out and freely began spreading the news of what Jesus had done for him.

Do you remember in some of our stories that Jesus mentioned a person's faith when they were healed or their sin forgiven? At another time Jesus had just finished telling a story about two builders, one wise and one foolish. He was now in a city. There was a foreign soldier's servant who was highly valued by his master the soldier. The servant was sick and about to die. The soldier heard about Jesus and sent some of his Jewish friends to Jesus to ask that he come and heal the servant. When the friends came to Jesus they pleaded earnestly with Jesus saying, "This man who is a foreign soldier deserves to have you do this. He loves our nation and people and has even built us a place for worship." So Jesus went with the friends.

When Jesus was not far from the house the soldier sent more friends to Jesus saying, "Lord, don't trouble yourself, for I do not deserve to have you come under my roof. That is why I did not consider myself worthy to come to you. If you will just say the word, my servant will be healed. For I am a man under authority, with soldiers under me. I tell this one, 'Go,' and he goes; and that one, 'Come,' and he comes. I say to my servant, 'Do this,' and he does it."

When Jesus heard these words of the soldier he was amazed. Jesus turned to the crowd of people following him and said, "I tell you. I have not found such great faith even among my own people." The men who were sent to Jesus returned to the house and found the soldier's servant healed.

Do you remember the story of blind Bartimaeus who called out to Jesus for help? As Jesus and his disciples were leaving a certain city, a large crowd was following. Along the way sat a blind man named Bartimaeus who was begging. When Bartimaeus heard that it was Jesus who was passing by, he began to shout, "Jesus, have mercy on me!" Many of the people in the crowd rebuked Bartimaeus, telling him to be quiet. But Bartimaeus shouted even louder, "Have mercy on me!"

128

Jesus heard Bartimaeus' shouts and stopped and said, "Call him."

So the people called to the blind man saying, "Cheer up! On your feet! He is calling you." Bartimaeus threw his cloak aside, jumped to his feet, and came to Jesus.

Jesus asked the blind man, "What do you want me to do for you?"

Bartimaeus said, "Lord, I want to see."

"Go," Jesus said, "your faith has healed you." Immediately Bartimaeus received his sight and followed Jesus along the road while praising God. When the people saw what happened, they also praised God. That is the story from God's Word.

Comfort the Heart:

1. In each story what did the people do who needed help? Who did they go to or send for?
2. What did Jesus do? Did Jesus want to help the person in need?
3. In the story of the man with leprosy, what did the man say to Jesus? What did Jesus say to the man? What else did Jesus do to the man?
4. When Jesus touched the man, what did that say about Jesus? Would you have touched the man?
5. In the story about the soldier's servant, why did the soldier send his friends to Jesus instead of going himself?
6. Then when the soldier sent more friends to Jesus what did they say? Did the soldier believe that Jesus could just speak the word and his servant would be healed?
7. When blind Bartimaeus cried out to Jesus, did Jesus hear him? What did Jesus ask Bartimaeus to do? What did Jesus say healed Bartimaeus?
8. What lessons have we learned from these stories about asking God for help?

Remember the Blessing:

"Let us then approach the throne of grace with confidence, so that we may receive mercy and find grace to help us in our time of need" (Hebrews 4:16).

HOPE Stories

34. Thanking God for His Help

Scripture Base: Luke 17:11-19; John 12:1-8.

Stir Their Thinking:

1. Among your people, when someone helps you, how do you thank them? What is an appropriate way to show that you appreciate their help?
2. How do you feel toward a person that you help but they never return to thank you?
3. If you ask God to help you, would you want to thank him?

Tell the Story:

Thanking God for His Help

Once when Jesus was traveling along the border between his home and the neighboring province he entered into a certain village. Ten men who had leprosy were there to meet Jesus. They stood at a distance and covered their faces as their law required and called out in a loud voice, "Jesus, Master, have pity on us!"

When Jesus saw them he said, "Go, show yourselves to the priest as a testimony of your cleansing." And as the ten lepers went to do what Jesus commanded, they were healed and made clean.

One of the lepers, when he saw that he was healed, came back, praising God in a loud voice. He threw himself at Jesus' feet and thanked Jesus. Now this man belonged to a group of people that many considered to be of low caste.

Jesus asked, "Were not ten cleansed? Where are the other nine? Was no one found to return and give praise to God except this foreigner?" Then Jesus said to the man, "Rise and go, your faith has made you well."

131

Do you remember the sisters Mary and Martha who had a brother named Lazarus that Jesus raised from the dead? Shortly before the time that Jesus was crucified he arrived in Bethany where Mary and Martha and Lazarus lived. There was a dinner was prepared to honor Jesus. Martha was serving the food while Lazarus was with the guests at the table. Then Mary came bringing a jar of expensive perfume and poured it on Jesus' feet and wiped his feet with her hair. The house was soon filled with the fragrance of the perfume.

One of the disciples named Judas, the one who was later to betray Jesus, objected. "Why wasn't this costly perfume sold and the money given to the poor?" he asked. Judas did not really care about the poor for he was a thief, while he carried the money purse for the disciples, he often helped himself to the money.

"Leave Mary alone," Jesus replied, "she has saved this perfume for the day of my burial. You will always have the poor among you, but you will not always have me." That is the story from God's Word.

Comfort the Heart:

1. Being a leper in the day of Jesus was a serious matter. You were considered unclean and worse than any animal. You were like a living dead person.
2. How do you think the ten lepers might have heard about Jesus?
3. Do you think they believed Jesus could heal them? What did the lepers say to Jesus?
4. What did Jesus ask them to do? What happened when they went to obey Jesus?
5. How many returned to thank Jesus?
6. Why would Mary and Martha want to honor Jesus?
7. What special thing did Mary do to honor Jesus?
8. God's greatest gift to us is eternal life through Jesus.
9. What would you do to thank God for His wonderful gift and for His gracious help?

Remember the Blessing:

"...always giving thanks to God the Father for everything, in the name of our Lord Jesus Christ" (Ephesians 5:20).

Chapter 6

Drawing the Net and Saving the Catch

Preparing to Draw the Net:

For those on short term assignments you may not have the opportunity to be the one to draw the net. Nevertheless, you should be prepared to do so if listener response and opportunity permit. Otherwise, you will be preparing listeners for local national workers or resident missionaries to draw the net at the right time. Your preparation will therefore be crucial. It is not uncommon for some listeners to need a processing time after hearing these stories. This is the time that the Holy Spirit deals with an individual's heart.

There are really three essentials. First is your own readiness through prayer and concern for the people you are serving. Second is a combination of biblical knowledge and preparation to teach that knowledge in a listener-friendly manner. Third is the relationship that comes through your sharing the Bible stories, building listener trust, and leading them to discover what God is saying about their relationship to him as sinners needing His forgiveness and mercy.

It sometimes happens even early in the story series that some listeners may be moved to respond by asking what they must do. Be prepared to take them aside as privately as you can and share a more direct witness presentation using your favorite evangelism scriptures or witnessing tract. As you are able to lead responsive listeners to faith in Jesus be sure to remind them that others are not yet ready to make the same decision.

Drawing the Net:

We use Bible stories to capture listeners' attention and hold it while we tell the stories to teach that we are all accountable to Creator God, that because of sin we are under God's judgment, and that God has prepared a substitute sacrifice for us who is Jesus. So there is a progression. We don't begin with the story of Jesus or with Jesus' death on the cross because they may not be ready to hear it or may yet believe that it is only a story for Christians. So by telling the stories in a progression there is opportunity for listeners to "buy in" or to position themselves relative to the stories. When telling the Bible stories we always have in mind where listeners are spiritually at the moment and where they need to be in order to make a profession of faith in Jesus.

One thing that Westerners need to know is that many in other parts of the world people do not make individual decisions alone. They make decisions in a group or community setting or at least with the approval of the community. For this reason it is important for the community also to hear the stories so that hopefully all the listeners are at the same point spiritually. It makes it much easier for responsive people in the group to profess their faith.

Another thing is that due to persecution or fear of it that some will be very reticent about making any public profession of faith. Whether you agree or not it does happen that people make decisions and choose not to tell anyone, biding their time until they feel it is safe to reveal their heart. This has been true among women in the Muslim world. While it is important for listeners to be challenged to make a positive response to the invitation for salvation, the Bible storyer will need to be sensitive to the best way to do this culturally. If you don't know, find someone who has lived among those people who can help you do what is culturally appropriate and most likely to encourage the desired response.

Saving the Catch:

There are several things that will help to save the catch. One is to develop a leader that you can share with and teach as much as they can learn while you are with them. It is an investment that will continue to pay dividends. Pray with that person and especially for them after you leave.

Another way is the Scripture verses that listeners learn after the stories that can continue to bless them as they recite the verses from memory and share the verses with others.

Gather the new believers and those who are seekers into a group so they may strengthen one another, pray together, recall the stories they have heard, and sing songs that praise God and His Son Jesus. This could begin as a fellowship group and progress into a worship group. There is strength in numbers, especially among those of new faith.

If there is time and opportunity, read or share some of the stories from the Book of Acts about the New Testament Church and what the believers did after Jesus returned to heaven.

Count on persecution coming in various ways. You can use some stories like those in the Book of Daniel, or in Acts like those of Stephen, Peter and John, Paul and Silas. Remind the new believers that Jesus is the Good Shepherd who is able to keep his sheep (John 10).

They must live holy lives that honor God (1 Peter 1:13-23). We know that anyone born of God does not continue to sin. (1 John 5:18) Jesus told his disciples: If you love me, you will obey my teaching. My Father will love him also...(John 14:23).

Ask the listeners if there are things in their lives that do not honor God, things they need to confess and change. There are many issues that you could explore related to charms, idols, the matter of forgiveness, doing what honors God and not what is often done to defend or uphold family honor by way of revenge or retaliation.

Nonliterates can have a daily quiet time by recalling the Bible verses or stories they have learned and asking God to help them live by God's Words. And always remember to thank God for His help and blessing.

135

Encourage the new believers to tell the stories to others in their families, their neighbors, and, when there is occasion, in other villages. The stories are kept alive by being exercised or retold.

If you are with semiliterates or literates and you have some printed discipleship materials you can share these as well and take the time to go through the materials and explain any teaching that is not clear to them.

Some simple discipleship lessons are "What Jesus Wants His Disciples to Know and Do" by LaNette Thompson (biblestorying@sbcglobal.net). These are eleven lessons based on the Gospel of John. The purpose is to help new believers and those who want to know more about what it means to follow Jesus to understand some of the teachings Jesus gave his disciples: What Jesus wanted them to know and what Jesus wanted them to do. To download a copy: (www.cbstorying.com), select "Methodology," "Story Sets," "Discipleship and Leadership Training"   and scroll down to "What Jesus Wants His disciples to Know and Do."

For more thorough discipleship story lessons go to the *Following Jesus Series* website: http://www.fjseries.org/low/home.html.

And with all, take time to have some fellowship and sharing in the name of Jesus. Share your testimony and let them share theirs. Commit them to God's care as you leave.

May God bless and strengthen the helpers who go to give hope to those in great physical and spiritual need and the stories they will tell to proclaim the beautiful message of the Lord Jesus.

Chapter 7

Resources for Your Bible Storying

I will offer to correspond with any of you who would like to prepare to use Bible stories during your ministry times. If there are questions about choosing stories, preparing stories or telling stories during an anticipated time of assistance, let me know and I'll try to help you find an answer. If you love God's Word and value it, if you love the people where you go to help, then take the time to share those precious stories as part of your ministry during their time of need.

Keep a diary of your Bible Storying experiences and your worldview notes. These may be very helpful to others.

If you want to read more about Bible Storying and what results various ones are having, in your internet search engine type in "Bible Storying" or "Chronological Bible Storying" and see what comes up. Several websites feature additional resources. Also check the Global Recordings Network (http://globalrecordings.net/topic/storytelling) and the Campus Crusade Storyrunners for additional examples of story use. (http://www.storyrunners.com/)

For general Bible Storying resources, go to: (www.cbstorying.com)

For Bible Storying, orality and training. Also be sure to check the Links in the sidebar for many websites that are related to orality and use of Bible stories. (www.oralstrategies.com)

The text *Basic Bible Storying* covers the basics of the methodology, preparing your stories for telling, and some of the various strategies of successful use in the chapter on The Bible Storying Toolbox. (www.churchstarting.net)

Additional resources are at God's Story (http://www.gods-story.org/) and audio Bibles at Faith Comes by Hearing (http://www.faithcomesbyhearing.com/).

Bible Storying newsletter is a quarterly e-publication with brief stories and reports of Bible Storying news that is safe to share, occasional mini-case studies, ideas for developing Bible Storying ministries, training, and resources. The newsletter began in 1994 and is published in January, April, July and October. Subscribe at: Biblestorying@sbcglobal.net.

Specific counseling, consultation and recommended resources are available from me via email at no charge. My personal goal is not in promoting a particular method of teaching or sets of Bible stories, but in being a part of seeing that all peoples have access to and opportunity to hear God's Word in a manner they can understand, respond to, and share among their own people. We do the work, taking advantage of every opportunity. The Holy Spirit brings conviction of sin and urges hungry hearts to respond to Jesus as Savior.

References

[1] Caloy Gabuco, "Telling the story," New Tribes Mission/ International Mission Board, SBC. http://www.ntmbooks.com/index.jsp?categoryid=61.

[2] J.O.Terry, *Water Stories from the Bible.*, JOT2@sbcglobal.net.

[3] J.O.Terry, *Grief Stories from the Bible.*. JOT2@sbcglobal.net.

[4] J.O.Terry, *Food Stories from the Bible.*. Available late 2008.

[5] Disaster Assistance Response Training (DART), Strategic World Impact. www.swi.org.

[6] J.O.Terry, *Basic Bible Storying*, Church Starting Network. www.churchstarting.net.

[7] MegaVoice players are digital solid state handheld players that have a solar recharger. www.megavoice.com or info@megavoice.com.